A Pocketful of Possibilities
Impossible Dreams, Made Possible

Twenty years ago, I watched a young woman and my friend, Shuronda discover the Architect of the plans for her life (Jeremiah 29:11). As a result, she has written "A Pocketful of Possibilities: Impossible Dreams, Made Possible." This book will illuminate the path that will lead you through God's plan for your own life and dreams. Relax, read and listen! Change for your life is inevitable!

Pastor Kathy Hayes, Founding Co-Pastor
Covenant Church, Carrollton, Texas

You may not know it, but God is working on you right now. This book in your hand is part of His strategy. Whether you are waiting on a dream to be revealed, or trying to revive a dead one, *A Pocketful of Possibilities* is for you. Shuronda Scott has captured the essence of what it means to begin to dream again. Prepare to be encouraged and empowered as you learn how to believe in your dreams again, remain steadfast through long seasons of waiting, and how to walk in the fullness of your dream released. As Shuronda shares in her book, *your dreams aren't just for dreaming, they are for fulfilling.* I guarantee you will be transformed, as you arise and start walking in your "possibilities" today!

Kerrie Oles, Author of the book, *Invisible Chains* **and Founder of Living Divine Ministries, Dallas, Texas,**
www.livingdivine.org

Shuronda Scott has an extraordinary ability to draw out the dreams that lay dormant in individuals. In *A Pocketful of Possibilities*, Shuronda reveals steps to unlocking those dreams. This is a must read for individuals of all ages who need help discovering God's plan for their lives. The message she shares in this book will remove limitations, bring freedom and confidence to release your dreams and will put you on the journey to fulfilling God's purpose.

Carolyn Gilleylen, Director of Women's Ministry
Grace Outreach Center, Plano, Texas

Shuronda has always been a passionate woman with a strong determination in helping others realize their dreams and goals. In *A Pocketful of Possibilities*, she navigates you through the painful loss of shattered dreams, and helps you discover the gift and power of God's amazing healing and restoration that releases you to dream again. You will be inspired and challenged by her ministry of hope that points you to a loving God who heals, restores and makes what seems impossible...possible.

Ricky Texada, Pastor
Covenant Church, Colleyville, Texas

In her book, *A Pocketful of Possibilities,* Shuronda inspires readers to believe in the dreams God has placed in their hearts. She gives us courage to step out on the promises of our Father. Through her insights and stories of challenge and triumph, she helps us understand that our dreams and purpose do not have an expiration date. I believe God is using Shuronda to stir up dreams that have been lying dormant inside us all.

Derozette Banks, Senior Pastor
Overcomer Covenant Church, Seattle, Washington

Shuronda Scott is a voice of wisdom, encouragement and inspiration. *A Pocketful of Possibilities* is based on years of her own personal experience and success with her many clients. You will become activated in a whole new way as Shuronda gives you a plan of action for imagining the possibilities and making your dreams reality. Read it and expect to be challenged, treasured and changed!

Jill Hellwig, Co-Author of the book, *When Women Reign* and Creator of the Brand New U System

Shuronda Scott's book will inspire and move you to follow your dreams! *A Pocketful of Possibilities* is a must read for anyone who wants more for their life and is ready to take action to get it!

Thank you Shuronda for your inspiration of hope and happiness on this journey through life!

Michelle Prince, Best-Selling Author of *Winning In Life Now*, www.WinningInLifeNow.com

A POCKETFUL OF POSSIBILITIES
Impossible Dreams, Made Possible

SHURONDA SCOTT

A Pocketful of Possibilities
Impossible Dreams, Made Possible
www.walkinginpossibility.com

Copyright © 2012 by Shuronda Scott

Published by 10 Talents Media Group
2810 Trinity Mills Road #209-274
Carrollton, Texas 75006
www.10talentsmediagroup.com

Printed in the United States of America

All rights reserved. This book or parts thereof may not be reproduced in any form, stored in a retrieval system, or transmitted in any form by any means—electronic, mechanical, photocopy, recording, or otherwise—without the prior written permission of the publisher, except as provided by United States of America copyright law.

Unless otherwise noted, all Scripture quotations are from the New King James Version® of the Bible. Copyright © 1979, 1980, 1982 by Thomas Nelson, Inc. Used by permission. Scripture quotations marked (NIV) are from the Holy Bible, New International Version®. Copyright © 1973, 1978, 1984, International Bible Society®. Used by permission. Scripture quotations marked (KJV) are from the King James Version of the Bible. Scripture quotations marked (NLT) are from the Holy Bible, New Living Translation Version. Copyright © 1996, 2004, 2007 by Tyndale House Foundation. Used by permission of Tyndale House Publishers, Inc., Carol Stream, Illinois 60188. All rights reserved worldwide.

Emphasis within scripture quotations is the author's own.

International Standard Book Number (ISBN): 978-0-9852961-0-0
Library of Congress Control Number: 2012903954

Cover design by Lotteice Greene, Ultimate Element Design Co.
Cover photo by Jen Sulak, Pink Light Images Photography
www.pinklightimages.com
Cover model, Karla Armstrong, CEO of mommyStrong™
www.mommystrongdfw.com

Dedication

To my Heavenly Father, my Lord and Savior Jesus Christ, my One true desire and Hope of glory.

Thank You for loving me with an everlasting love and for making impossible dreams possible in my life.

Acknowledgements

I want to thank my mom who has always believed in me and been my biggest fan no matter what I have endeavored to do. Even though, we never talked about our dreams, her confidence in me inspired the hidden dreamer in me to reach for the impossible.

I want to thank my two wonderful brothers, Steaton and Garrick. You are amazing men and becoming great men of God with incredible opportunities and possibilities yet to be discovered.

To my beautiful niece, Tatum "Jewels", may God give flight to all your dreams...you were born to soar. Keep dancing!

To my dad, I thank you for allowing God to do a complete healing and restorative work in your life that has given me the opportunity to get to know the wonderful man that you are. Your story proves that God loves to redeem and make the impossible possible in our lives. God has only begun to use you.

To Stephanie Lebeauf, I could not have done this without you. Thank you for your invaluable collaboration throughout this process and the needed accountability that encouraged me to write. I have grown so much and cherish every moment of sharing the countless hours of inspiration and ideas back and forth. Everyone needs a friend in their *myPossibility* network like you.

To Faye Wright, your encouragement and many years of support speak volumes. You know what you mean to me. You were the catalyst that opened the way for many possibilities from the moment you called me your "sister in Covenant."

To Pastors Jerry and Jessye Ruffin, your mentorship and spiritual insights helped me recognize and remove the ashes in my life that unveiled the greatest possibilities and potential (within) and the opportunities (without). I am forever grateful.

To Pastors Ricky and Cyd Texada, thank you for your mentorship over the years and even to this day. I am proud to have been a part of your team. You believed in the gift in me and released me to soar. Your mantle of leadership impacts countless thousands within and outside of Covenant.

To the many women who have dreamed alongside of me encouraging me with your powerful stories of dream fulfillment and loving support: thank you to Tami Chalhoub, Gail Davis, Tedeen Franz, Judy Horton, and the Women's Ministry Leadership Team. I want to give a special thanks to Karla Armstrong. It has been amazing to see God orchestrate and unfold His incredible possibilities in our partnership. May your picture go around the world!

To my editing team, Louvenia Freeman, Jessica Julian, and Felecia Okpagu, you have been awesome. I also want to give special thanks to Heather Fitzgerald, Jackie Shepherd and Earma Brown for providing invaluable feedback.

I want to extend a special thanks to my pastors, Mike and Kathy Hayes for their spiritual leadership and for allowing me to serve and grow in my gifts over many years. My possibilities expanded the moment I stepped through the doors of Covenant Church.

Pastor Amie, thank you for your creative inspiration and confidence in me. When you speak (in your teaching or your books), people do listen and they are greatly impacted. I know I have been! In fact, the title *A Pocketful of Possibilities* was through your inspiration.

Contents

Foreword		13
Preface		15
Introduction:	I Dreamed a Dream	21
Chapter 1	Pile of Dreams	27
Chapter 2	God's Plans for Your Dreams	41
Chapter 3	Standing at the Crossroads of Shattered Dreams	55
Chapter 4	Dreams That Live Again	85
Chapter 5	Impossible Dreams Made Possible	107
Chapter 6	Taking Your Dream Out of the Wait	113
Conclusion:	Your Dream Made Possible	135
	End Notes	143
	About the Author	145

Foreword

The entryways to the impossible are rarely found in the predictable patterns of our lives. So much routine catches us in deep grooves of the probable. But there are distinct ways of escaping the mundane and launching into the miraculous. Books are the most dependable method I have found of entering THE place of eternal purpose where possibility is opened up before us. My positive experiences, with reading my way into a realm of *"what if"* is most likely what led me to write five books of my own. You see, when we find the fold in the golden curtain that boxes us all in, we crave the opportunity to share an insight, create a map for others, in the hope that all may find their way through the impossible. I have known Shuronda for more than twenty years. And in that time, it has been everything from exhilarating to excruciating to watch her push through, carving a path for us to follow. When the impossible pushed her, she pushed back. And I am honored to say that she has found THE pocket and charted a course for us to access the possible! Reading this was not only enjoyable for me but extremely inspiring and motivating! As I finished the book, I feel as if I've been deep in the pocket that I only just found on the first few pages. My pockets are full! I believe yours will be as well. Be prepared, when you dive in, possibilities pour out!

Amie Hayes Dockery, Senior Associate Pastor, Covenant Church, Carrollton, Texas and Author of the recently released When Women Reign and others

Preface

Little did I know the unfolding path that God had designed for my life and the dreams that He had planned for me. I didn't know then the countless number of lives that I would be able to influence and impact for His glory. All I knew that day was that my shattered dream of serving God in ministry, and being used by Him to do great things lay at my feet. I was emotionally broken, defeated and disillusioned; and I had no hope of my dream ever coming to pass.

Young and passionate, my dream pursuit was to serve God in full-time ministry. I had only recently moved to Dallas after graduating from college. I was working successfully in the accounting profession, developing tax software for accounting firms and corporations. Life was good, but I knew God was drawing me into a deeper place in Him, and that He had something for me. As I was praying one day, I asked the Lord, "What is it that You want me to do?" As I persisted in prayer, the scripture in Luke 4:18 came to my mind.

> *"The Spirit of the Lord is upon Me,*
> *Because He has anointed Me*
> *To preach the gospel to the poor;*
> *He has sent Me to heal the brokenhearted,*
> *To proclaim liberty to the captives*
> *And recovery of sight to the blind,*
> *To set at liberty those who are oppressed;"*

What did the Lord mean by this? Had God called me to preach the Gospel, and to bring healing to the brokenhearted? Who were the brokenhearted? I felt a tremendous stirring in my heart that continued to grow, but no one in my family had ever been called to ministry. In fact, in my church denomination, I didn't know of any woman that had been called into ministry, so this was all very new to me and hugely intimidating. All I knew was that God wanted to use me in ministry, but how would I ever get to that place.

No, I did not fully understand all that He had for me, nor what I would have to walk through to step into it. I could not have imagined the storm of emotional and spiritual torment over the next few months that would bring me to this crossroads, and what I thought was the death of my dream. I had given up all to pursue God. I had quit my job. I had given up my apartment. I had decided to pursue the call of God upon my life by going to seminary. Going to seminary was a big step. I didn't know how I would pay for it, or even how it would come about...it was a giant faith step.

During this time, I had also become a newly spirit-filled believer, and was learning to follow God's voice and direction in a whole new way. My intimate relationship with the Lord grew tremendously, and I was experiencing new spiritual levels in my faith. I also experienced an increasing level of spiritual warfare for which I was completely unaware and was poorly prepared. I lacked the spiritual understanding of the tormenting battle that raged against my spirit and mind. I realized for the first time that I had an enemy intent on stopping the plan of God for my life.

I had fasted and prayed for months and I thought I had a plan. However, I struggled with confusion and doubts, and wondered *did God really call me to ministry* as the doors weren't opening. Why weren't things working out the way I thought? My plans for seminary didn't materialize, and I learned some important lessons about God's timing and His preparation. I know now that God allowed this time of testing in my faith, as well as used it to teach me many things about spiritual warfare that I have used over the last twenty years in ministry.

Standing at my crossroads confused and broken by life's circumstances and things that didn't work out the way I thought; I questioned, "Lord, what do I do now?" I was afraid and unsure about everything. I felt as though I was holding on by a thread to the promise that I am *kept by the power of God through faith (1 Peter 1:5)*, but did I have enough faith? What I didn't know at twenty-five (that I now know over twenty years later) was that I wasn't holding onto God, He was holding on to me, and He had the power to deliver me from my strong enemy. Maybe in your dream pursuit, you have come to what seems like a dead end. The enemy sent his best shot to derail you, but God Almighty has a plan.

I received two words that day, "Go back!" I had left everything and I thought *how would I be able to return?* Within a few minutes of getting up from that time of prayer, I had called my old boss to express that I would like to come back to work. God's favor is so amazing. In an instant, He opened the door for me to return to my job with a comparable salary as before. I even called the apartment complex in Dallas, Texas where I had lived, and the manager said they had one apartment to lease and it was mine if I desired it. In one day (actually a few hours), God turned my crumbled circumstances around and restored ALL that was lost.

The biggest restoration would come in me. You see, I had stepped out boldly in faith believing that God had called me to do great things for Him. In returning, I felt like a failure, broken and defeated. The dream in me was crushed. Fear took hold and so gripped my life that I became very afraid to step out there again to do anything for the Lord. I didn't want to mess it up. I struggled with this until one day God spoke to me and said, "I'm bigger than your mess ups. Don't you know that I've ordered your steps and that I have a plan to prosper you?" That began the healing process from what I thought was my biggest failure and test of my faith at the time. Tonight as I write these words, I'm reminded of a song which was led by one of our beloved worship pastors, Sally Ayers, who has since gone on to be with the Lord. It was titled, *Lord, You Have Been Faithful to Me."* How the words to that song soothe my heart and calmed all my fears during many dark nights. That day, I laid on the altar the ashes of fear and failure, and the broken ministry dream somehow trusting. I said out loud, "God, You're still in this, I trust You."

I remember the encouragement of one of my dearest friends and, a true sister in Covenant, Faye Wright who walked through the spiritual, physical and emotional storm with me. She said to me comforting me, "One day, you're going to look down, and the huge gash on your leg will be all healed and you'll have only a small scar. And you are going to wonder how did that happen?" She was right. God's healing and restoration is so complete, so thorough, so redeeming. Psalm 18:50 has become a life scripture to me, and I often declare it in first-person. It is the same Psalm David spoke when God delivered him from the hand of all his enemies.

"Great deliverance You give to *(Your servant, Shuronda)*
and how You show
mercy and love to Your anointed, to *(Shuronda)* and *my*
descendants forevermore."
Psalm 18:50 *(italics, emphasis added)*

I knew that God had a purpose for me and He had called me to do something great for Him. I surely didn't know all it would cost me. But it was well worth the miracle of healing and restoration and seeing impossible dreams made possible in my life. It was worth seeing the ministry that was birthed in and through me and the opportunity to have served Him now for over twenty years.

We all have incredible dreams that God wants to fulfill. Maybe you have yet to see your dream come to pass. Maybe you stand at a crossroads today and you feel your dream is dead. Don't give up. I have seen many desires and dreams fulfilled in my life. I'm still standing on the promise of others. God wants you to know that you have a *pocketful of possibilities* as you walk with Him. He is able to take your dream that seems impossible and make it possible. Discover for yourself all that God has for you. The dreams that you have are His impartation to your destiny. Don't lose patience or let your hopes become dim. I promise you, you are going to be amazed!

Introduction

I Dreamed a Dream

*S*he walked onto the stage unassuming and grateful to be there. She was just herself, but the audience's response was less than receptive. No one knew the journey she had taken and the circumstances surrounding how she even came to be standing there on that stage that day. She was a woman just like you and me, very ordinary...who had lived a life up to this point, quite mundane and simple by the world's standards. Yet, she had a big dream. Nervous and somewhat shy, she stood before the famous and world esteemed panel of judges...taking in the incredible moment.

She was asked the question, "What is your dream?" She responded that she would like to be able to sing like one of England's music greats, Elaine Page whom she had been inspired by throughout her life. The audience, looking only at her appearance erupted with murmurs of doubts and disbelief, until she opened her mouth to sing in the most beautiful, melodious voice the song, *I Dreamed a Dream.*

It was a breathtaking performance that silenced every critic and stunned the judges sitting before her, rather I should say amazed them. Yes, *I Dreamed a Dream* was the song that catapulted an unknown woman the world now knows as Susan Boyle onto the international scene. In fact, videos of her performance and rendition of the song, *I Dreamed a Dream* went viral on the internet reportedly garnering over 100 million views within a week. She became a singing sensation overnight.

I am really not a big reality TV fan, so I didn't watch Susan Boyle during her debut on *Britain's Got Talent*, but you couldn't help but hear about her superstar rising that caused her to become known far and wide. I'm intrigued and moved by her story as I think we all are. That day was a moment in time in which unfathomable opportunities and possibilities opened up and were released for her. Her path had taken her from pain to fame it seems almost overnight.

The biggest miracle of all about her story was the message in her song, *I Dreamed a Dream.* The moment this 47 year old ordinary looking woman from Blackburn, West Lothian, Scotland stood on that *Britain's Got Talent* stage, she released her life message to millions of onlookers and rekindled for us all a hope in dreaming again and is an example for all who are still waiting on their dream, that it is never too late for the fulfillment of your dreams. Today, she is living her dream, but it didn't start in that one day.

Introduction: I Dreamed a Dream

Although, you will read great stories of others and their dreams, this book is about YOUR DREAMS! It is written to those who have placed their dreams on a shelf or in a drawer somewhere, waiting to be fulfilled. It is about how to take your dreams out of the wait and to begin living in them now. It is about discovering the unfolding possibilities God has for you in the fulfillment of your dreams.

For many, even as it was for Susan Boyle, you may have come to a crossroads of what seems to be shattered dreams as she experienced when her mother died (her debut on *Britain's Got Talent* was supposed to be her last performance in honor of her mother). This book is for you. It is about restoring and resurrecting dead dreams. It is about overcoming the discouragement and pain of hope deferred. It is about turning the pile of "dream ashes" that may lie at your feet (as it did mine) into beauty again.

A Pocketful of Possibilities – Impossible Dreams Made Possible is written to walk you through different seasons in your dream pursuit and right into walking in the incredible reality of all God has for you.

Chapter 1 Pile of Dreams calls you to remember your dreams again. For some this is remembering dreams you thought were lost. For others this is giving yourself permission to dream, even if for the first time. It is about reigniting, rediscovering and reawakening your dreams, hopes and vision.

In **Chapter 2 God's Plans for Your Dreams**, you will discover the purpose and the plan God has for your dreams and why He desires your dreams to be fulfilled more than you do.

Chapter 3 Standing at the Crossroads of Shattered Dreams helps those who may have confronted life crushing circumstances and events that leave you confused and broken over a shattered dream. It reveals the dream ashes that can bury your dreams and how you can rise from the pile of ashes. Discover how God turns all of the ashes of our broken dreams into something of beauty when surrendered to Him. Your dream is never discarded; it's only refined to bring God glory.

Chapter 4 Dreams That Live Again is about recovering all that was lost in the valley of dream despair. Watch as God breathes on the ashes of your dead dreams causing them to live again. You can receive healing for the brokenhearted dreamer within and discover a newfound faith and strength to conceive and release the impossible made possible in your life. Your God is the God who still speaks to dead wombs!

In **Chapter 5 Impossible Dreams Made Possible** you'll discover that there is nothing too hard for God to do. For with God, all things are possible to him who believes.

Chapter 6 Taking Your Dream Out of the Wait is about learning how to live in the dream right now. It's time to dust off your dreams and go for it. Step onto the stage of possibility. God has unfolding possibilities and opportunities for you to realize your dreams. You will learn how to create your own roadmap of possibilities to your pathway of greatness. It's all up to you; take your dream out of the wait, now!

Thank you for allowing me to share highlights from my life with you on this journey. Writing this book has been one of the richest experiences I have encountered and has been one of many dreams to finally see fulfilled. I have discovered expanded possibilities to my dreams, a deeper place of vulnerability as well as unlocked areas for greater personal healing by sharing my story. I pray you are blessed by it.

Read on with me. When we get done, you're just going to look back at where you were and wonder "How did I even get here?" It's going to be exciting. Remember your dreams aren't just for dreaming, they are for fulfilling. You will see your dreams unfold as you discover and walk in the amazing *pocketful of possibilities* God has for your life right now. Start walking in possibility today!

Chapter 1

Pile of Dreams

*"The stars exist that we might know how high
our dreams can soar."*

I took the decorative box off the shelf and opened it up. I poured the contents out into a pile on the floor and began to go through each folded up slip of paper. Each piece that I unfolded represented the hopes, dreams and desires of hundreds of women who attended our church conference that year and who had participated in my breakout workshop session.

God had spoken to my heart the morning of the conference and told me to tell the women to take their dreams out of the wait. The box was a demonstration of how we allow all of our hopes and dreams to be stuffed away in an old drawer or box sitting on a shelf collecting dust.

At the beginning of the session, I asked the ladies to take a few minutes to write down the hopes, dreams or desires that they desperately wanted to see fulfilled in this season. Once they had finished, I asked each lady to place their dream or dreams in the decorative box.

Permission to Dream

It is amazing to see the delight that comes through when we are given the opportunity to consider our dreams. It is like the delight I see on the faces of children when they dream and imagine. I still remember a couple of the women saying, "Hold on" as they wanted to be sure to get their dreams placed in the box. It was great fun and required for each of them to engage and to think about what they really wanted. For some it was remembering how to dream and allowing themselves permission to dream.

I had asked them to consider and write down the desires from childhood, things they may have forgotten until now, things they had simply discounted, the things they thought impossible. It was an exercise in releasing their faith to believe and for some to believe again and most importantly for them to believe now. God wanted to take their dreams out of the wait for them to walk in now. As we finished the session that day, we took the box of dreams and prayed God's word and release over all the hopes and the desires it represented. It was powerful. God spoke and declared to us that day, "I'm blowing the dust off of your dreams today, and I'm releasing you to start living them today!"

Dream Pursuit

When I began writing this book, I wasn't sure what direction it would take. I had a couple of book projects that I knew God had impressed upon me to move forward on and to begin writing now, but which one? All I knew is that I needed to write, so write I did. Forty pages into writing, I asked the Lord. "What am I really trying to say and more importantly, what are You desiring to say through me?" You see, writing a book has been one of my dreams for many years. I felt overwhelmed and pressured in some ways just to complete the goal. This particular day, I stopped and realized, silently praying: *Lord I'm not going to be able to do this without You. Help me! Where do I begin?* At that moment, God reminded me about the decorative box of dreams sitting on my shelf. It had been over a year since the conference, and I still had this box full of the hopes, dreams and desires of my sisters along the journey. As I pulled out and read each piece of paper, I was deeply moved and wondered about the unfolding path for each woman in her dream pursuit. Was she walking it out as God had prophesied and encouraged that Saturday morning?

Many of the women had dreams to move into ministry. Some wanted to start their own business. Others desired to write a book. One woman wanted to run a marathon in the seven continents. Another wanted to build a music museum for children. Still others had dreams of restoration and healing for their families. However, one of the slips of paper included four words that grieved me. It simply stated: "To have a dream."

Overwhelmingly, and I think surprising to me, many of the women wanted to be married and have children. Wow, I didn't realize that in that small box were hundreds of dreams and many of them very similar. Of my own dreams included in that box that day was my desire to meet and marry the man God has prepared for me and to have children. When I got to this little slip of paper with a familiar handwriting, I knew this was the one I had placed in the box that day.

So Whatever Happened to Your Dreams?

Walt Disney was a man who accomplished great things in his life. A great businessman, animator, film producer and imagineer who brought to life great classics and heartwarming family films and movies like *Mickey Mouse, Treasure Island, Mary Poppins, Bambi, Cinderella and Snow White* and the *Seven Dwarfs*. I still remember as a young girl watching these great movies that made me laugh, cry and laugh again. All of them characterized with an uplifting message of truth and good overcoming evil. Disney movies were heartwarming and magical and made me dream. What young girl doesn't dream of her knight in shining armor or a prince that would come and sweep her off her feet? Yes, what fun! Disney created magic and through his imagination, he caused children and even us "big kids" to dream. In fact, his name and legacy has be-

come synonymous with "magic" and "making dreams come true." Walt Disney was a dreamer, and through his dreaming he built *Disneyland*, the most successful theme park in history, now with several locations throughout the world. Passionate about education and art training,
Disney also helped establish the *California Institute of the Arts*, a college-level professional school of all the creative and performing arts. His inspiration was to provide a place where students of different art forms could develop their talents, dream together, and create a mixture of the yet unimagined needed for the future.[1]

Walt Disney conceived the unimaginable and his creative magic forever lives to inspire others to realize their dreams today. He built a great legacy that still influences and inspires millions of lives all over the world. He saw the impossible made possible in his lifetime.

Unfulfilled Dreams

I shared earlier with you about the woman who said that she would just like to have a dream. I have pondered those words written on that small piece of paper. What could she mean? Did she mean that she has never had a dream and would like to have one? Perhaps she had one that didn't turn out the way she thought it should...it was shattered by crushing life circumstances or a devastating event. At any rate, here she was attending yet another conference, sitting in my session and she wasn't sure now how to move forward. I don't know what state, emotionally or otherwise, she was in that day. Whatever she thought left her, dream unfulfilled and hopeless. I know that it broke my heart as I read those four little words, "To have a dream." And I believe that it broke God's heart and breaks His heart today that His children do not know how to dream or do not give themselves permission to dream.

The Lost Art of Dreaming

Dreaming is allowing your imagination to soar and I believe it releases the creative side that is most like God. Take Walt Disney for instance. His artistic talent was a God-given gift and he used it to do incredible things in his day. As he shared his plans and his dreams, he was often mocked or told that it couldn't be done, that it was *impossible*. He was quoted as responding: "It's fun to do the impossible." Well, what do you know? Who does that sound like?

"With men this is impossible, but with God all things are possible." (Matthew 19:26)

It's time we believe and conceive. It's time for us to dream again!

During this writing process, I asked family and friends lots of questions. The main one was, "What did you dream about when you were a child?" I asked my mom, what did she dream about when she was younger? She responded that she really didn't remember having dreams as a child. She only remembers that she and her older sister, my Aunt

Jimmie would talk about growing up, getting married and having children. That was her dream perhaps. Did she simply not know how to dream? What about you? Do you allow yourself to dream? Are you teaching your children how to dream?

I remember many years ago coordinating a week-long discovery camp for four or five young girls. It was a summer retreat with fun activities geared toward developing and building a positive self-esteem.

During one of the group activities, I asked the girls to each share what they wanted to be when they grew up. One shouted out "I want to be a teacher!" Another exclaimed, "I'm going to be a singer!" When I got to the next young girl, she timidly shrugged her shoulders and sheepishly said, "I don't know." I said, "I'm sure you've dreamed of something, it can be anything." "Nothing", she responded. My heart broke and I realized that she had never been taught to dream. Even today, I encounter children and adults alike who do not have any dreams.

Hearing this young girl's response helped me recognize that when people do not dream, they settle for whatever their environment or previous experiences dictate. They settle for less and they fail to realize the fullness of the purpose for which they are designed. Now after many years of coaching and counseling people, I have discovered how true this is.

At that point, I decided that I could help make a difference. I wanted to expand their ability to dream, to inspire them and to enlarge their experiences. So the next year I used my airline miles to fly the girls on their first airplane flight to their nation's capital, Washington, DC.

Just as we see through Walt Disney's life, God has planted dreams deep inside your heart that perfectly fits the person you are. He wants to give flight to your dreams so that He might release the fullness of His purpose in and through you.

This book is about unlocking your dreams. It's time to dream again and it's time to realize your dream. You just might be the next Walt Disney! Don't you agree, "It's fun doing the impossible!"

I want you to really allow yourself to dream. Don't allow yourself to be limited by your current surroundings, experience or background. Just dream!

Go Ahead, Release Yourself to Dream

You probably remember hearing as a kid, "Stop your daydreaming!" Whether it was a gentle prodding from a parent or teacher to refocus, to finish your homework or to put away those foolish notions, those three little words, in many ways, have stifled the creativity God has placed within us.

As children, we learned there were far more important things to think about, like going to work so that you could put food on the table. So, who has time for dreaming of any kind? Especially if it is that whimsical pastime of daydreaming often viewed by the culture around us as just plain laziness or being non-productive.

Like many others, you may have heard comments such as:

- *You don't have time for that...it's not going to pay the bills.*
- *That just an old pipedream, you'll never be able to do it.*
- *No one makes a living doing that...*

And the list goes on. Over time those words have proven to thwart, limit and inhibit our ability to release ourselves to dream. Although unintentional, permission to dream was slowly eroded away.

We have allowed the culture around us to pervert the true definition of daydreaming; which has been termed as mindless wandering. God desires to infuse us with the ability to dream (even if in the daytime) about the possibilities that He has for us.

"...eye has not seen, nor ear heard, nor have entered into the heart of man, the things which God has prepared for them that love him." (1 Corinthians 2:9)

Although balance is important for children who daydream, I believe they should be taught how to dream and while they are at it to DREAM BIG! It is time for us to recapture the art of dreaming and to release ourselves to dream big.

"Expert Dreamer" by Tami Chalhoub

I used to daydream often as a child. What would my husband be like, what kind of career I would have, what kind of mom I would be. It was almost daily. I created vivid pictures in my mind about my future, and it was always grand.

Somewhere along the way, I stopped dreaming. We are told to be realistic, get our head out of the clouds, as if there is something wrong with living among the clouds. Over time, life gets in the way, and we are so focused on the here and now, that we don't have time to think about what lies ahead. I don't want that to happen to my children, I pray that they never stop dreaming.

I watch my nine-year old little girl. She is what I'll call an expert dreamer. At such a young age, she has set huge goals for herself, and they're specific. She wants to start her own fashion line, live in Paris and New York, sing and win Grammy's, act and win an Oscar, just to name a few! She has even broken her dreams down into time-bound goals. In five years, she wants her business to move into its own building; in 7 years, she wants to have her own TV show. Those are big dreams! I have to be honest. Initially, the "realist" in me, would try to steer her to narrow her dreams. I thought to myself, what are the odds that she can actually achieve all of that? I thought if I were realistic with her now, it would save her disappointment later.

I thought I was helping her. What I was actually doing was lowering her sights. I heard myself talking to her one day, and couldn't believe the words coming out of my mouth.

"But sweetie, it's really hard to do that..." Why limit her? Why limit what God can do in and through her? If a dream is not just a little hard to do, it's probably not a big enough dream. And where was my faith? As she gets older, and discovers the gifts God has given her, God will help shape her dreams to line up with what He planned for her before she was even born. In the meantime, I encourage her to keep dreaming. I want her to continue to be that expert dreamer. The world needs more of them.

Now we have fun conversations at bedtime. She describes the apartment in New York that she is going to live in, and I close my eyes real tight and picture it with her. When she asks me if I think it's possible, I tell her, *"Oh yes, sweetie, and then some!"*

Giving yourself permission to dream is only the first step. One of my favorite authors, Dondi Scumaci describes another challenge of truly releasing yourself to dream in her book, *Ready, Set...Grow!*

"Many of us are just too busy to dream.
We have a dozen must-dos, and dreaming never quite
reaches the top of the pile."[2]

God gave us dreaming as a tool to move us toward success. Our dreams truly are the vehicle that motivates and moves us toward the incredible, unfolding opportunities and reality that God desires for us. Dreaming is allowing yourself to consider the new possibilities that God has for you. Dreaming is simply reaching for more. It's about allowing yourself to dream of what can be different in your life today.

The next step is making time to dream. I want to encourage you to find a quiet place and spend some time focusing on your dreams and what *you* want for your life. Like me, you may need to ask yourself the question, "What dreams have I been too busy, too afraid or too disappointed to pursue?" My prayer for you is simply this: May you conceive the unimaginable and release its beauty to the world for God's glory. Dream!

DREAM TIME: *Creating Your Dream Journey Moments*

The following questions may be used to spark your dream time moments.

1. If you could live anywhere you wanted, where would it be? Describe what the place *(or home)* would look like.

2. If you could do anything, no matter how risky, and you knew you couldn't fail, what would it be?

3. Name one person that you would most like to meet.

4. Write down a place that you would like to visit one day, another city, state or even a different country. *(I recently decided that I wanted to visit Disneyland of all places! So give yourself permission, it might be fun.)*

5. What job would you do if resources *(i.e. time, money, etc.)* weren't a concern or limit?

6. What would you like to change about the world around you?

7. What is the one dream for your life (your deepest desire) you most look forward to having come true? Think for a moment, what would that look like? *(If you are having trouble with this question, look back over the previous questions and see if there is a pattern or theme.)*

Chapter 2

God's Plans for Your Dreams

> *"For I know the plans I have for you, declares the LORD,
> plans to prosper you and not to harm you, plans to
> give you hope and a future."*
> *~ Jeremiah 29:11 (NIV)*

I was talking to a friend one day and she said that she rarely dreams when she goes to sleep at night, and that if she did, she couldn't remember them. I often dream, and sometimes they are very vivid, significant dreams. And at other times (as I know many of you may have experienced), I have had a few dream-tossed nights that are very likely the result of the giant stuffed pizza from the evening before. In any case, most will agree that dreams are intriguing. So whether you are one who dreams a little or a lot, when you lay down to sleep at night, be assured that your dreams do matter.

As I was discussing this fascination with another friend, I paused and asked, "What do you dream about?" She shared that she dreamed about her life or people in her life. Sometimes, she dreamed about her two young children and what their lives would be like when they grew up. At other times, she would dream about the challenges and concerns from the day that she had of necessity carefully stuffed away in her now cluttered "subconscious drawer." I can definitely relate.

These were often the things...the fears, the doubts, or the relational conflicts she wasn't quite ready to face or deal with. Most often God would use her dreams to confirm things that He had been speaking to her heart.

As she openly shared how God would sometimes use her dreams to affirm and reaffirm His will and purpose, I was reminded of another young dreamer in scripture. I thought about how God used his dreams to reveal a great purpose and plan for his life and not for his purpose alone, but his family and his entire nation. Yes, I'm talking about none other than *Joseph, the Dreamer.*

God: The Dream Giver

For many years now, Joseph has been one of my favorite Biblical characters. He has been referred to in many children's Bible stories as *Joseph the Dreamer* because of his dreams as a youthful boy.

Chapter 2 ~ God's Plans for Your Dreams

Joseph had a dream, and when he told it to his brothers, they hated him all the more. He said to them, "Listen to this dream I had: We were binding sheaves of grain out in the field when suddenly my sheaf rose and stood upright, while your sheaves gathered around mine and bowed down to it." His brothers said to him, "Do you intend to reign over us? Will you actually rule us?" And they hated him all the more because of his dream and what he had said. Then he had another dream, and he told it to his brothers. "Listen," he said, "I had another dream, and this time the sun and moon and eleven stars were bowing down to me." When he told his father as well as his brothers, his father rebuked him and said, "What is this dream you had? Will your mother and I and your brothers actually come and bow down to the ground before you?" His brothers were jealous of him, but his father kept the matter in mind.

~ Genesis 37:5-11 (NIV)

Joseph often gets a bad rap for being overly ambitious, prideful even, daring to dream or believe that his brothers and even his father and mother would one day bow down and offer him homage in some way. However, I see someone who was willing to dream something that was so far-fetched, something that was so incredibly implausible, that it would take only God to accomplish. Joseph dreamed big! And whether he realized it at the time or not, his dreams were the God breathed seeds of inspiration of the great things He had planned for his life.

His story is one of exaltation and a miraculous rise in influence and power. We might call it a great success story, a coming out of nowhere (an obscure life of insignificance...remember Joseph was a slave in a foreign country) into that of greatness (fame and the powerful influence that saved a nation). It is also a story of reconciliation, restoration and redemption for his family and his own nation. Yes, God unfolded a great plan for Joseph's dreams. Joseph saw his implausible or should I say impossible dream made possible in his life.

The Inspiration of Dreams

Throughout scripture, we see how God has used dreams in many ways. Some of the remarkable instances of how God used dreams include:

- *To reveal and confirm His will (Paul – Acts 16:9)*
- *To encourage (Gideon – Judges 7)*
- *To reveal the future (Joseph – Genesis 37:5-10)*
- *To instruct (Joseph & Mary – Matthew 2:13)*
- *To warn or restrain from evil (Abimelech - Genesis 20:3)*[1]

I believe God uses the creative language of dreams that are released through the overflow of the Holy Spirit in our lives. In the book of Acts, the Apostle Peter spoke of this creative overflow when talking about the outpouring of the Holy Spirit upon the disciples who had gathered in the upper room.

Chapter 2 ~ God's Plans for Your Dreams

> *"And it shall come to pass in the last days, says God, I will pour out of my Spirit upon all flesh: and your sons and your daughters shall prophesy, and your young men shall see visions, and your old men shall **dream dreams**."*
> *(Acts 2:17)*

"Your old men shall dream dreams." The overflow of the Spirit of God poured out upon our lives releases us to dream dreams, to see visions and to prophesy what God is speaking. I believe that our dreams and desires are most often inspired by God and flow from the creative side of who He is. Dreaming is just one way of awakening this creative language that unlocks and connects us to yet unrealized possibilities that God has for us.

Does God still speak to us through dreams, vision and prophesy today? Absolutely, and more importantly, I believe God wants to awaken our faith, creativity and imagination to believe Him for more...the impossible, the incredible dreams, plans and purposes that He has for our lives. The scripture says "your old men shall dream dreams." It is interesting to note that it says "old men will dream dreams." Our ability to dream doesn't ever stop. God put within us the capacity to dream and to continue to reach toward the greater dreams and visions that He has for us, for our families, our businesses, our ministries and more.

God uses our dreams to motivate us toward the things He has called us to do.

A Pocketful of Possibilities

To dream is not just something we do when we fall asleep at night. I'm referring to our ability to let our imagination soar, to conceive and to envision the expanding possibilities and great things God has for us.

Walt Disney was a man who let his imagination soar. In fact, one of the things said of Walt Disney is that he was an "Imagineer." Imagineering has become synonymous with the Walt Disney Company. The term also describes the skill set embodied by the employees of WDI, known as Imagineers.

"Walt Disney Imagineering (also known as WDI or simply Imagineering) is the design and development arm of the Walt Disney Company, responsible for the creation and construction of Disney theme parks worldwide."[2]

I absolutely love this term. Imagineering is the blending of two words: imagination and engineering. Although, today it is used most often when speaking of the company built by Walt Disney, "Imagineering" was made popular in the 1940's by ALCOA who described it in a 1942 Time magazine article as follows:

"Imagineering is letting your imagination soar and then engineering it down to earth."[3]

Walt Disney was a man who completely embodied this creative language. In the biography of his life, it is said that Walt envisioned the new theme park: Walt Disney World EPCOT Center later built in Florida on his hospital ceiling. Although, he didn't live long enough to see the completed themed-land park that bears his name, he imagined it and spoke it into being. We get a glimpse of Walt Disney's imagination and vision for the future that he continually engineered down to earth, making his dreams a reality.

Ask yourself are you an Imagineer? Are you a dreamer like Joseph? When it comes down to it, dreaming is about expanding your capacity to believe that God's plan for your life can be great.

Fulfillment of your dream is God's greatest desire for you.

Your visions, hopes and dreams are important elements toward God's amazing plan for you...*a plan that includes a glory-filled earth through each of you.* God's glory is going to be revealed through you, and He gave dreams to you to produce it. Why wouldn't He want to fulfill them?

Joseph's dream was about exaltation; a dream of greatness; that God was going to use him in a great way. God's plan included using him as a great leader and deliverer. The dream was not just about his father and brothers bowing down to him. It was about ruling and reigning and being positioned to administer the multifaceted plan, rule and authority of God in the earth. As a result of his dream fulfillment, he changed the lives of many individuals along the way and influenced a nation for eternity.

How do we begin to live out our dreams, realizing our dreams are for now and not later? What are some of the things we have to do? God will always provide a focal point like He did with Joseph that was relatable to him...a dream seed. His dream wasn't just about his fathers and his brothers. It was much bigger than that. Just like your dreams are!

God starts it by planting a seed in your heart of where you are going to be in the future.

He then releases you to start walking it out. Did Joseph understand the dream seed God had placed in his heart? Much like us today, I'm sure there were times when Joseph wondered if his dream would ever come to pass. Through every pitfall and prison stop, Joseph walked out his dream. There was nothing that could stop the fulfillment of his dream because God had a plan all along.

That's what I love about the story of Joseph. God even used the most difficult of circumstances to bring about his dreams and to ultimately produce His will in Joseph's life.

I believe that God's design for our dreams always includes what is being produced in the unfolding process of realization. Joseph evidenced this in how he lived; what he did; and how he progressed. God's original blueprint for him was to live successfully; transacting business in the realm of everyday life. Our original blueprint is also a design for success in whatever we do.

I tend to be very practical, and I equate the practicality of life with living in the spiritual...for it is in Him (Jesus) that we live, move and have our being.

What did Joseph do?

I believe that he recognized his gifts and talents. He honed them and excelled at them. Whether in Potiphar's house or prison, he walked in his gifts continually. Joseph discovered a *pocketful of possibilities* that moved him toward the unfolding realization and expected hope of God's plan for his dreams. You can too!

So, God imparts dream seeds. The Bible also encourages us to *write the vision and make it plain so that we might run with it*...and as we are running, we somehow step into the all-encompassing, unfolding fulfillment of the things God has for us.

God Uses Everything To Bring About Your Dreams

Returning to Dallas, after stepping out into ministry, was one of the hardest things I have had to do. I felt like a complete failure, broken and defeated. Had I missed God? What did it mean now? Did He have a ministry for me? I returned to the last place of God's clarity.

I was thankful to have family and friends around me who knew how to pray. They were a huge support as God brought healing emotionally and spiritually.

I struggled greatly with fear, and there were times when I wasn't sure if God was speaking or if it was just me. So, when the Lord spoke to my heart and told me it was time to move to a new church...Covenant Church, I resisted. I didn't want to make a mistake or be out of God's will ever again.

I submitted what I thought was the next step to my pastor, and he confirmed that he believed it was God's will for me. What was God doing? I didn't know at the time, but He was positioning me for even greater possibilities than I had yet imagined and for greater development for the ministry call He had placed upon my life.

Many times in your dream pursuit, you may feel like you are starting over. I have discovered that God even uses times of setback and uncertainty to bring about His glorious will for your life.

In The Progress, There is Hope

Transitioning to a new church allowed me to connect in a new way with fresh vision and new relationships for my life. Even in my job role, I felt God was saying "It's time." But, time for what! I remembered the ministry call God had given me, but I wasn't really sure what to do with it. In bold faith, or perhaps I should say reckless faith, I had up and quit my job once before. Did I dare do that again?

I sought counsel and wisdom about what I was feeling...about the rekindled dream seed of ministry God had placed in my heart. I was encouraged by my pastor as she admonished me to stay put for now. Those words "don't quit your job" were sound and practical wisdom indeed, as I didn't have another job. And was I prepared for that step again? I knew that I wasn't. I was definitely still a little gun-shy about stepping out in faith again. I had done that only to be broken and defeated. However, as I look back now, I realize that God knew my heart, my desires....and

Chapter 2 ~ God's Plans for Your Dreams

my dream. He knew that I wanted to serve Him in ministry more than anything and with all my heart. In fact, He had put it there. He had planted the dream seed in my heart just as He has planted the seeds of dreams in your heart. God also knew the fear and doubts in my heart. I believe my pastor's words were sound advice, and more importantly I sensed the guidance and encouragement of the Lord directing my heart. It was as though, He was steering me down the path toward all the He had for me.

As my pastor counseled me, she asked if there were other opportunities for growth or something new that I could do at the company where I worked. The things that she said in that meeting that day opened my heart to new, unconsidered possibilities. As I left her office, I prayed a simple prayer, "Lord, would You open up an opportunity for me to flow in the gifts and anointing You've placed in my life."

A few months went by when I saw on our company job network a new job post for a Training Specialist. I knew that job was for me. It would allow me to develop and hone the speaking gift that I believed God had placed in my life. I was ready for something new, so I applied for the job. I did not get the position. It actually went to one, of my colleagues, who is a very good friend.

Of course, I was a little disheartened, but happy for my friend. It turned out to be a good thing. Because of my friendship with her, it allowed me to develop relationships with those in the training area and to expand what I call today, *myPossibility network*. Did God have a plan? Discouraged, I wasn't sure at this point.

A couple of months later, another training position came open in the same department. I was considered for the job since I had previously applied for the prior position. Like Joseph, God's favor opened the door, and I stepped into the preparation ground for the unfolding purpose of more than I had yet conceived.

The plan of God is always unfolding. Seven years after what I considered my biggest failure, I transitioned from my corporate job into full-time ministry. What I now know is that God was marrying my dreams with His divine purpose. God does have a plan for our dreams, and He will use our hope and desires to steer us toward the best that He has for us.

What Happens to Your Dream Seeds?

Dreams are thoughts visualized in sleep...the revealed thoughts of God to us that come in the form of dreams...

As I have richly discovered in my life, the *God-said* over our lives and the *God-breathed* dream seeds are God's thoughts that He imparts to us, about us, about who we are, about His plans and His will for our lives.

Jeremiah 29:10 declares: "For I know the plans (thoughts) I have for you says the Lord, plans to prosper you (thoughts of peace) and not to harm you (not of evil) to give you a future and a hope."

Plans refer to something that God has worked out in advance or has arranged for you.

Chapter 2 ~ God's Plans for Your Dreams

I love this scripture, and over the years I have grown to love it even more. The original King James Version of the Bible helps us understand in a greater way what God desires for us.

If you re-read the scripture "For I know the thoughts I have for you...you could very well say "For I know the *dreams* that I have for you...*dreams that release you into (bring you into) a flourishing, thriving, profitable, growing place* and plan that I have for you. God wants this for you *now*...not later. It is time to step into the fullness of the dream and purposeful plan God has for you.

The word "thoughts" is more powerful and speaks of the creative ability; the creative dimension of God that produces possibilities that are yet to be discovered so that you begin to live out your dream every day.

God wants to release other facets of the dream that maybe you haven't seen before today. Things that will give you permission to start living it rather than waiting for albeit something magical to happen.

God's Thoughts Toward You

Have you ever considered, *what are God's thoughts toward you?* If you are like most, you will probably agree that you have spent more time thinking about what others think about you rather than God. We all want to be thought well of. The biggest challenge can be what you think about yourself. Do your thoughts agree with God's thoughts for you? God reflects on you continually as declared in Isaiah 49:16, and His thoughts toward you are precious *(highly* valued and esteemed thoughts of your good—Psalm 139:17). So why not consider God's thoughts toward you. As we shift our thinking, and align with God's thoughts about us, we will begin to see all of the possibilities, opportunities and plans He has designed for us.

"Many, O Lord my God, are Your wonderful works which You have done; And Your thoughts toward us cannot be recounted to You in order; If I would declare and speak of them, they are more than can be numbered." (Psalm 40:5)."

MEDITATION MOMENT: *Aligning Your Thoughts With God's Thoughts*

Remember God wants far more for you than you know! Spend some time over the next week meditating on the thoughts He thinks toward you.

- God's thoughts are higher than your thoughts! *(Isaiah 55:9)*
- God's thoughts of you are unlimited! *(Psalm 40:5)*
- God's plans and the creative power of His thoughts are continually unfolding yet unrealized possibilities. *(Psalm 139:16)*

As you daily meditate on God's Word, you will discover the incredible plans He has for all your dreams and the amazing purpose He's laid out for your life.

Chapter 3

Standing at the Crossroads of Shattered Dreams

*"He gives beauty for ashes and the oil of
joy for mourning."*
~ Isaiah 61:3

We all have come to crossroads in our dream pursuits. What you thought would work out one way, but did not. Circumstances and situations out of your control brought about a different outcome than what was expected. So, where you stand today is a crossroads. In many cases, there are negative and even tragic events that have propelled you to this spot. Maybe it was the death of a loved one, or a divorce after many years of believing God for

A Pocketful of Possibilities

restoration. It might be the sacrifice of putting your education or your career on hold yet again or the disappointment over years of delay despite your prayerful petition for the Godly mate and children you have long desired. Oftentimes the crossroads in life are the adverse occurrences that come to thwart and steal the dreams that you have for your life.

Such was the case as I spoke with one of my dear friends, Gail. She was planning her very first conference at a leading resort hotel in the Dallas/Fort Worth area. In fact, the conference's theme was "Living Your Dreams." She had asked me to be a part of her conference as a speaker, and I was so honored to do so. We discussed her vision and her heart for what she'd like to see God do during this time. Her desire was to see women ministered to who had been waiting a long time on their dreams and those who had given up on their dream.

As we sat there in that restaurant, my friend talked about her dreams of ministry and ministering with her husband, who had died a few years earlier. She shared how broken and devastated she was when her husband passed away.

She had walked through much over the years: childhood abuse, a struggling marriage, and finally her husband's battle with congestive heart failure. She had even laid down her career to move away from all she knew to a small town to take care of her estranged husband. What a sacrifice.

Through the storm of adversity, God gave her a word that He would use her in ministry, and that she would min-

Chapter 3 ~ Standing at the Crossroads of Shattered Dreams

ister with her husband. When her husband died, she thought, *what about God's word to me? What about my desire and dream?*

That day in the restaurant as Gail shared what she had walked through the last few years, she spoke something so powerful. She said that as she was walking through this very painful time, questioning God about His promise of her ministering with her husband, a friend encouraged her with these words: "Who says that it's going to be this husband? You are young, and God's plans for you are still good, plans to prosper you and to give you a future and a hope."

So I celebrated with Gail as she launched her ministry and conference. As she stood on the platform of that stage, she had truly become a trophy of amazing faith and a grace-filled example of God's extraordinary restoration and power. He had renewed her hope and released her dream in a greater way than she had even imagined.

The message of this book is that God doesn't forget you. He hasn't forgotten your dreams. Just as He has revealed in Gail's life and my own life, He has a *pocketful of possibilities* for your life. So you may be standing at the crossroads of shattered dreams; things that have gone awry; wrong turns along the pathway of decision and more. God wants you to know that He has a glorious plan to redeem your yesterdays; restore your hopes and resurrect the dreams that you can live in today!

At the beginning, we introduced several women with big hopes and dreams just like you and me. As I have sifted through those nameless little scraps of paper, I discovered how much our dreams are alike.

A Pocketful of Possibilities

We all desire ministry or in other words the significance and the opportunity to do great things for God. We all want meaningful relationships either to be married and have a family or to have a better and successful relationship with our husband and children. We all want to be productive and leave a great legacy through building a successful business, writing a book that tells our story that perhaps changes the lives of those around us, or just using our creative talents and gifts.

Most of all, I discovered how each woman desired more for herself than her current reality presented. This was the common thread throughout the many dreams that were written down that day during our women's conference.

Over the last few weeks and months, I have wondered about the many dreams that I have spoken out and prayed for asking God to bless and to bring to pass every desire. The dreams may represent nameless faces to you and me, but they are very much written in the heart of God for each of these women. Those dreams have been recorded for eternity, but a nagging question loomed in the back of my mind, "Where are these women in their dream pursuit and fulfillment today?"

I recently read an article that only about three percent of people, accomplish their goals in life and ultimately, their dreams. As I thought about that for a few moments, I realized that of the two hundred women who placed their dreams in that box that day, only six potentially would live out the fullness of their dream. What about the other ninety-seven percent? What keeps them from living out their dreams? What keeps them from realizing the eternal reality God has recorded for them in the heavens?

Many things come to bury our dreams. One of my favorite authors, Dondi Scumaci describes it this way in her book, "Ready, Set...Grow!"

> "Distractions that come in life or simply inactivity have a way of coming in and choking the life right out of your dreams."[1]

What we find is that we are no longer heading in the direction of our dreams. Over time, through distractions and the adverse winds of trials, for many, the pile of hopes and dreams becomes a pile of ashes, or what I call "dream ashes."

Dream Ashes

The image of a pile of ashes reminded me of the destruction and devastation of that fateful and tragic morning, which brought change to many individual lives and our nation. It was September 11, 2001 and the world had just witnessed one of the deadliest terrorist attacks in history on American soil. Many lives were lost that day and the lives of families were changed forever. As I watched the television with my co-workers in the office, we were all stunned and sat in silence, eyes glued to the images of the events that we saw unfolding before us. As we prayed for our nation, we tried to make sense of those last few minutes, trying to understand what had just happened. While watching

A Pocketful of Possibilities

the rescue efforts, we were still trying to comprehend when the unthinkable happened...on live television right before us, the horrific collapse of the towers of the World Trade Center in New York City. With mouths wide opened, we watched as one camera captured the deep roar of the building crashing to the ground and then the rising, smoke-filled cloud of dust and ashes that erupted through the streets covering everything in its path. Images of the ash covered faces of stunned survivors emerging from the cloud of smoke and debris burned deep in my mind then and even now.

Surrounded by the ashes, we mourned as a nation the lives of many men and women that were lost that day.

Now over ten years later, as a nation, we looked back and remembered. Yes, it was a very sad day in our nation and a time of great mourning. As I recalled the events from that day, the symbolism of the ashes became even more real. The catastrophic events from that day affected the lives, the hopes and dreams of families and loved ones who remained. While not by choice, their hopes and dreams had in an instant become a pile of burning ash and rubble. Yes, it was at this dark crossroads in our nation's history, that for many the pile of twisted steel and debris had become a pile of "dream ashes."

Webster's dictionary defines ashes as "ruins; remains left over after something has been destroyed."[2] But what does "ashes" mean for you and me, and how do they affect the dreams that we have for our lives? The first thing I thought about was how the children of Israel covered themselves with "sackcloth and ashes." Throughout scripture,

Chapter 3 ~ Standing at the Crossroads of Shattered Dreams

ashes were often used to signify a time of mourning as in the death and loss of a loved one. Ashes were also used to symbolize sorrow and humility, represented in fasting and repentance (Daniel 9:3).

The children of Israel would cover themselves with sackcloth and ashes as a representation of the deep distress, grief, sadness, anguish or bitter sorrow of heart they were experiencing. In the book of Esther, chapter 4, I'm sure you can sense along with me Mordecai's deep anguish and emotional distress after hearing about the threat of death and annihilation of his own people. Mordecai was a Jew and cousin to Queen Esther who he had raised as his very own daughter. Haman, one of the King's officials and an enemy to the children of Israel plotted to destroy them by manipulating the King into signing a law to kill all the Jews. This was indeed a time of deep distress and anguish.

- *When Mordecai learned all that had happened, he tore his clothes and put on sackcloth and **ashes**, and went out into the midst of the city. He cried out with a loud and bitter cry. (Esther 4:1)*

- *And in every province where the king's command and decree arrived, [there was] great mourning among the Jews, with fasting, weeping, and wailing; and many lay in sackcloth and **ashes**. (Esther 4:3)*

Tamar, the daughter of King David, placed ashes on her head to signify her intense grief and pain over having been violated and wrongly disgraced by her half-brother,

Amnon. Her sorrow was so deep that she went away crying bitterly. The ashes of rejection and betrayal, covering her wounded heart, left her stripped of her purity and her hope.

- *Then Tamar put **ashes** on her head, and tore her robe of many colors that [was] on her, and laid her hand on her head and went away crying bitterly. (2 Samuel 13:19)*

Whether through death and loss, heart-wrenching disappointments or other painful circumstances and situations, there are ashes that can bury our dreams if we allow them.

As I pondered "dream ashes" more, the scripture in Psalm 102:9 really stood out.

"For I have eaten ashes like bread, and mingled my drink with weeping,"

The children of Israel were demonstrative in their mourning as depicted by the rending of their garments, sitting and laying in sackcloth and ashes. They generally would not eat or wash themselves during their grief period. They would mourn for a time and then the mourning would end.

As I meditated on this scripture, God gave me this image of a woman standing by an uncovered grave that represented all her hopes and dreams. She was still wearing the black sackcloth and ash covered funeral garments. With this reflection in mind, an old familiar phrase came to my

Chapter 3 ~ Standing at the Crossroads of Shattered Dreams

memory. "Ashes to ashes, dust to dust." It is a phrase taken from the English burial service prayer and is used to indicate total finality. Like me, you may recall hearing these words at a funeral usually spoken during the graveside service.

The children of Israel most often put ashes on their head or sat in ashes, and would sometimes lay in them. But, the significance of eating ashes seems to represent something further. In Psalm 102:9, for the children of Israel, the ashes had become as familiar as the eating of their bread.

This sadly represents many today. I thought about how often the ashes and specifically the "dream ashes" become the focus and sustenance of one's life and sometimes, unknowingly, they have chosen to live standing beside the grave. Broken-heartedness has become as familiar as the bread you eat. Grieving has become as familiar as living.

Grieving is a process that should bring healing. God never intended for it to become a way of living. Why? Because Jesus died and took upon himself all of our grief and sorrows (Isaiah 53:3). It is okay to grieve and it's important to give yourself permission to do so.

Over the years, God has taught me how to grieve the losses, the disappointments and the heartbreaks in my life. God wants to walk you through the pain and bring healing to your heart to release you to truly live, to hope and to dream again. Are you still living out of the ashes and ruins of past disappointments and calling that living? How can you realize your dreams when you aren't even living?

How many of you are still standing in your black sackcloth and ash-covered grave clothes waiting with your yet unrealized dreams sometimes months, years, and even decades later...? If the ashes are what you continually eat, you will never realize your dream. It's time to recognize and remove the ash covered grave clothes.

Ashes That Bury Our Dreams

I know that when you come to a crossroad of shattered dreams, emotionally and physically it is very difficult to move forward. Amidst the pain you may be grappling with, the confusion in the "Why?", or the shaking in the loss, it takes every bit of energy to hold on to your sanity.

The ashes that bury our dreams can look like many things. As I have stood at my own crossroads of shattered dreams, here are some of the dream ashes that I have had to sift through.

- **Ashes of Disappointment** – *Can be described as a feeling of sadness or frustration resulting from being let down or the failure to attain desired hopes and wishes (generally resulting from unmet expectations; something hoped for that did not happen).*

- **Ashes of Despair** – *A profound feeling that there is no hope; exasperation; hopelessness; despondency. A feeling that something will or cannot change. (Psalm 42:5)*

Chapter 3 ~ Standing at the Crossroads of Shattered Dreams

- **Ashes of Discouragement in Delay** (of Deferred Dreams) – *A feeling of discouragement tied to an expectation of something happening within a certain time. For many women, this may include their view of their age in the timing of events in their life (i.e. marriage and children by the time I'm thirty, etc.).*

- **Ashes of Death and Loss** – *The heartbreak over the loss of a loved one; a spouse, a sibling; a friend. Regrets sometimes causes an individual to get stuck or overcome with feelings of guilt or even anger at being the one left behind. Other losses may include the loss of a relationship as in divorce or a betrayal that wounds and bring feelings of rejection and abandonment.*

- **Ashes of Doubt and Unbelief** – *A continual feeling of uncertainty or to think that something is unlikely to happen (especially for you). Distrusting the good things that God has for you.*

These are just a few of the ashes that can bury your dreams. Other ashes that can bury your dreams include the ashes of fear and rejection. Or maybe the ashes of guilt and shame keep you from realizing your dreams. For some, even the ruins and the devastation of past generations (family ties of brokenness, bondage or wrong beliefs) can try to bury your dreams. You cannot build your dreams on the rubble and ashes of past generations. Trust God to remove the ashes that are holding you back.

Trusting God has never been more difficult than when standing amidst the ashes of the death and loss of your dreams. It truly becomes a burnt offering and ashes of sacrifice unto the Lord. You don't have to allow these ashes to continue to bury the dreams God has for you yet to live. It is time to remove the black cloak of sackcloth and ashes. It is time to rise from the pile of ashes. Let God turn the ashes into something of beauty.

Which of these ashes are burying your dreams? There may be other ashes that God reveals to you. List them below:

_____
_____
_____
_____
_____
_____
_____
_____
_____

What Do You Do With the Pile of Ashes?

Many of you women know that once you reach forty your body begins to change. When I turned forty, I was still hopeful. Forty is a number for transition, and I felt God was ready to do some new things in my life. Surely, it

Chapter 3 ~ Standing at the Crossroads of Shattered Dreams

would be marriage, since I was anxiously longing to not only get married but also to have the wonderful children and family I had long desired since childhood. It was my dream. I had lots of other great dreams, yet this was still the ONE I longed for most!

My fortieth birthday came and went. It was a grand celebration with dinner at one of my favorite restaurants. I had lots of family and friends toast and roast me during the occasion. My mom, of course, had wonderful things to say about her favorite and only daughter. My two wonderful brothers, who had no idea they would have to speak on my behalf, were just as gracious. Wasn't it enough that they just showed up? Still, how their words and expressions of love melted my heart! Thank you, Garrick, and thank you Steaton for capturing this joyous occasion on video!

Well my fortieth birthday was great! It made me a bit reflective as I looked back over the years, the dreams I had seen come to pass and goals I had accomplished. But, there was still this ONE. It was the big one! "When, Lord? You know I'm getting older." Forty-one, forty-two, forty-three! "Oh God, what about my desire for children?"

With each passing year, my doctor would query in his soft-spoken way if there was anyone special in my life. He knew my desire to get married and have kids, and I reasoned this was his way of asking without being intrusive..."Do you still want to marry and have children?"

Although, I was hopeful, faith-filled and enthusiastic on the outside, underneath were the most painful heart moments of all each time I sat in my doctor's office watching the years slip away. Did I really have faith to believe God for all my dreams when the world tells you...*you're too old?*

I thought about God's word in the book of Joel.

"And I will restore to you the years that the locust hath eaten, the cankerworm, and the caterpillar, and the palmerworm..." (Joel 2:25a KJV)

Did I really believe that God would restore the years that I had waited on him to fulfill my dream and His promise? The sweet melody of one of my favorite songs, *"I Will Bless the Lord"* came to mind. With tears streaming down my face, I got in my car and drove away from my doctor's office that day. One phrase in the song encouraged me and brought comfort to the pain... that God is the *"mender of the broken, healer of the soul; redeemer of all yesterdays."*[3] My response through the tears was "Lord, I trust You and I live to glorify You, so I will bless You Lord at all times. Once again, I place my dreams in Your hands."

Trusting God

Trust God! We hear it often as an encouragement from others. I do agree that this ultimately is the place we all have to come to...where else could we go? Trusting God does not diminish the pain that results from a place of brokenness, dream shattering circumstances that come in our lives, like the death of a love one, the loss of a job, a very serious and life threatening health challenge or maybe a

Chapter 3 ~ Standing at the Crossroads of Shattered Dreams

dream deferred. Trusting God helps us to put our wounded hearts in the hands of the only One who can truly mend and care for it. The only One who can strengthen and encourage it!

> *"Wait on the Lord;*
> *Be of good courage,*
> *And He shall strengthen your heart;*
> *Wait, I say on the Lord!*
> *(Psalm 27:14)*

Over the last year, I have meditated on and thought a lot about the Biblical character, Sarah. I imagined that Sarah had to come to this same place many times. I know that over the last twenty years, I have been here many times and have had to ask the Lord to encourage my heart. Sarah walked through many, many years.

In Sarah's day, women had children very young. The struggle of barrenness, which was often viewed as a reproach, I'm sure, was very painful to her. At twenty, did she think, "When Lord?" just like I did or at thirty-five..."Okay Lord, where are You?" At forty-five, did she despair? She was a woman just like you and me with tender emotions and deep heart-felt desires. Put yourself in her shoes. At the time of the Promise, she was sixty-five. What did she think? Was she still hope-filled or was she grappling with the pain of discouragement and disappointment? It had been years of delay. Did she wonder how can this ever be? Did she feel forgotten?

The Bible tells us that Sarah received strength to conceive.

> "By faith Sarah herself also received strength to conceive seed, and she bore a child when she was past the age, because she judged Him faithful who had promised."
> (Hebrew 11:11)

God came through, encouraging her heart...just as it is promised to us in Psalm 27:14 which we read earlier. He strengthened her heart through faith as He will strengthen yours and mine today.

Believe God and trust Him today! Let your prayer be, even through your pain:

> "I would have lost heart, unless I had believed
> That I would see the goodness of the Lord
> In the land of the living."
> (Psalm 27:13)

When I have reached this place (and I have often), I have had to encourage myself in the Lord and remind myself of His promises to me. I do this by writing in a book (my personal prayer journal) all the things that God has spoken to me over the years. It may be a prophetic word or a scripture that God has illuminated for me. I start it off with..."Lord, You said..." It is like a book of remembrance of all the promises God has spoken. I go back to it and I remind the Lord of His word to me....not to anyone else but to me.

Chapter 3 ~ Standing at the Crossroads of Shattered Dreams

"This is what the LORD, the God of Israel, says: 'Write in a book all the words I have spoken to you. (Jeremiah 30:2)

Take a moment and remember the words that God has spoken to you. Write them here; then spend some time praying and meditating on His promises below. Allow God to minister hope to your heart about all that He has planned for you.

Words God Has Spoken to Me

_____

_____

_____

_____

_____

_____

_____

Promises of God that Cause Us to Hope

He has promised He will never leave you nor forsake you (Hebrews 13:5)
> *"...I will never leave you nor forsake you."*

He has promised you rest and fulfillment. (1 Kings 8:56)
> *"Praise be to the LORD, who has given rest to his people Israel just as he promised. Not one word has failed of all the good promises he gave through his servant Moses.*

He has promised you an inheritance. (Ephesians 1:11)

> *"In Him also we have obtained an inheritance, being predestined according to the purpose of Him who works all things according to the counsel of His will..."*

He has promised you that He has a plan for your life. (Jeremiah 29:11)

> *"For I know the plans I have for you..."*

He has made us partakers of the covenants of blessing and promise. (Ephesians 2:12-13 NLT)

> *"In those days...you did not know the covenant promises God had made to them. You lived in this world without God and without hope. But now you have been united with Christ Jesus...you have been brought near to him through the blood of Christ*

The Ashes of Sacrifice

Up until now in our journey, I have talked about the ashes that bury our dreams. Now I want to talk about ashes that will release your dreams to live. Sarah must have felt the same way we feel when standing at a crossroad of ash covered dreams. She was standing at a decision marker of having to willingly offer up the "son of promise" who had made her to laugh again.

We only see in scripture the response of Abraham, Isaac's father, but what about his mother, this woman who had waited on her dream all of her life. I'm sure, like most husbands and wives, they had a conversation or two on what Abraham said God told him to do. I can hear Sarah's words and prayer now to her God. "Are you sure, Lord this is what you want us to do? To take my only son and sacrifice him? This is the son I have waited on for ninety years. I'm way past a hundred now, Lord, and I know there aren't any options left for me."

Finally, as Abraham prayed and waited, Sarah came to the place of submission that she had learned to do...so many years and so many times before. "God is faithful, and I know I can trust Him." I can picture her the next day as she hugged her son and kissed him goodbye, willingly offering to God the sacrifice of her most cherished desire.

How many of you have come to the place where you believe this is the dream? At last! I have waited for so many years and finally I'm walking in it...but only to see it crumble around your feet.

A Simple Prayer

My prayer was a simple one that morning as I was preparing to go to church. During my quiet time, I had been expressing my thankfulness to the Lord for my dad and my two wonderful brothers. It was Father's Day, and I wanted to honor them. Over the years, they have been the men in my life. Well there has been one Man, my Lord Jesus, who I must praise and thank for who I am today and how He has blessed me with a wonderful family. So this morning, I was thanking God for all of His faithfulness to me and that I had the opportunity this Father's Day to celebrate with my dad and two brothers. I was also grateful for the many Spiritual fathers and brothers in Christ who have loved and been faithful to protect me as a woman, as a daughter, and sister over the years. As I think about it now, it was all about the men that day! As I shared my heart with the Father that morning, I said, "Lord, I'd really like to meet the man that you have prepared for me and get married." I had prayed for my mate many times before, but today was different.

Excuse Me, Where Are My Manners?

Sometimes, you are surprised by what you find right around the corner, or should I say, just through the door. That's when I bumped into my friend, Shawn. I had missed him over the last few weeks, and I was delighted to greet him and ask how his family was doing.

As I walked up to him, I realized I interrupted a conversation he was having with the person standing next to him. "Excuse me, I didn't mean to interrupt you." As I shook hands with the very gracious and rather handsome looking man standing close by, he said, "I know you." Surprised, I said "You do?" In the brief few seconds, a connection was made, and to my surprise a lunch invitation extended. And to my shock, an affirmative "Sure" was my quick response. Then, I thought to myself, *who is this guy and what did I just do?*

"The Dream" I Have Been Waiting For

Lunch that day turned into three amazing hours and I knew this was different. I had not dated in a very long time, and my discovery was...relationships are wonderful!

Chapter 3 ~ Standing at the Crossroads of Shattered Dreams

There is the excitement of getting to know one another, spending time discovering new things together, meeting each other's family, falling in love and then comes the big decision. Afterwards, there is preparation; there is work and learning how to grow together. Oh, did I say there is work? Yes, relationships are wonderful and at times quite challenging. I didn't realize all I didn't know, but I have grown so much personally, as a part of the process.

Meeting this special person was one of the most exciting things that had happened in my life. So when our relationship and plans of our upcoming engagement ended, it was very difficult for us both.

The most important thing I've discovered is learning how to trust God for His will and sometimes His timing in our lives. I'm reminded of a poem I read many years ago that included a line that says: "...but God says no, not until you are satisfied with me." What stood out is the "no, not until." Not until what...I had waited a long time. "Lord, wasn't this the dream that You promised?"

As women, it is difficult to understand, especially when we have fallen deep in love, and when things don't work out as planned. Sometimes, we are left wondering, *Okay Lord, what happened?* I thought this was the fulfillment of the dream. Yes, the relationship may have ended. Most women will probably agree that what ended was also their hope. Sometimes God has you to lay the promise down, to put it on the altar even when you don't understand.

God says, "My thoughts are not your thoughts, nor my ways your ways." His wisdom is infinite, and *His ways are past finding out* (Rom.11:33). He also knows what He is working in you and working out of you.

As I stood at my crossroads, heartbroken over the shattered dream that lay before me, I said, "Lord, I don't understand. What about your promise to me?" As I sought God, He simply said, "Trust me." It was the most difficult thing I've had to do.

Still, I am convinced that I would not be the woman I am today if God had not allowed this relationship in my life. The heartbreak and the crushing of my dream, after waiting so long for it, drew me closer to Him in a way that wasn't possible before. It also drew me closer to you, and helped me understand the brokenness of heart that so many have experienced. God's promise is that He heals the brokenhearted and binds up every wound. And in the process, your heart is strengthened as you wait upon the Lord.

The dream is not being discarded, it is only being refined.

No matter what the circumstance or situation you lay on the altar today, you have to trust God, whether he stays your hand, as in the case of Abraham and Sarah, or whatever outcome results. God is able to keep the promise He has made unto you.

After my relationship ended (the one that held all the hope of the promised fulfillment of my biggest dream), I asked the Lord, "Why did you allow this if it was just going to turn out this way? What about your word to me? I have not dated for twenty years. I have waited, and I was willing to wait longer...I think I was willing."

God gently spoke to me and said "Regardless of My word or what you thought about this situation, are you will-

Chapter 3 ~ Standing at the Crossroads of Shattered Dreams

ing to trust Me with the outcome?" "Yes Lord, I am willing." I didn't understand it. All I knew was that through the crushing, and the desperation of the pain, I was saying yes. I think I may have felt a little like Job.

"Though He slay me, yet will I trust in Him." (Job 13:15a)

For you, maybe it was a devastating divorce, or the loss of your job and dream home that resulted in your shattered dream. Maybe that ministry door didn't open up when you thought it would, what now? Sometimes, it's a business venture that doesn't work out the way you thought. You knew it was God's idea, so what happened? It just didn't work out.

Sometimes, we have to offer up on the altar our *dream ashes* for that business, ministry, and even that relationship in order to see the fullness of what God is bringing forth.

The beauty for ashes comes in the obedience unto the Lord. Either this is not the right time or God has a greater plan.

For You I Will

One day over lunch, I shared my story of heartbreak over the last year with a friend, and how the experience had changed me forever. How it has changed my relationship with God forever! She looked at me with eyes full of anticipation. "Wow Shuronda, I feel something big is coming.

She continued shaking her head, I don't know what it is, but it is big!"

God has to sometimes shake us loose of the dream we have held so tightly to, so that He can release the bigger thing, even a bigger dream. I know this book has become more personal, more vulnerable for me since walking through this wonderful experience. I'm not saying the pain was wonderful...I'm saying what it produced in my life was. Yes, my *ashes of sacrifice* have become something of beauty. It's the beauty that God has developed in me, and yes, it is the resurrected *hope* and expectancy of all He has for me! And now I know in a greater way the God who is able, and I know that *for me* He will do whatever he has promised!

Rising from the Pile of Ashes

Our team had just finished a powerful and sweet time of prayer during our monthly prayer meeting. Each time is always special, however today was especially sweet. The group was smaller than usual which provided a different intimacy in God's presence. As the ladies prayed individually, I began to sense a place of brokenness. I initially thought, "Is this just me?" I had been in a real place of brokenness, hurt and pain over the loss of what seemed to be fulfillment of the promise of the mate I'd desired for over twenty years. You see, I had purposely not dated before meeting this very special man. Well to be honest, I cannot say it was my purpose or plan. I had longed to be married way before now. Yet God had hid me away, and by design, He had not allowed me to even date anyone. My focus had been ministry and passionately pursuing the call of God upon my life. Yet, I deeply desired to be married and have a family. It has been one of my deepest longings and dreams that I have desired to be fulfill for many years now. So, what happened? Did I miss God? I had waited twenty years, but it seemed my relationship hopes had turned into a pile of ashes. So, that place of brokenness was very real to me, and I knew that I was sensing the same for many of the other women kneeling and praying in that room that day.

As I led the women in a corporate prayer time, I shared with them what I sensed the Lord was speaking. My encouragement and prayer for them that day is the same encouragement for you wherever you are today. God recognizes the place of discouragement and disappointment that you are in, and He has not forgotten you.

Brokenness comes in our life in so many ways. Life circumstances can blindside us and overtake us. You think you are living but you really aren't. God understands the pain and heartbreak. This place of brokenness for me was a broken engagement and a failed relationship. I was overwhelmed by the many mistakes I made along the way and the broken-heartedness as a result of my shattered dream. Your place of brokenness may be similar. It may be the result of loss, death, delay of His promises, a failed relationship, personal and moral failure, or physical challenges. No matter the broken place, God desires to heal.

His word says He heals the brokenhearted and binds up all their wounds. It is preeminent in Christ's mission and the purpose of why He came.

> *"The Spirit of the Lord God is upon Me,*
> *Because the Lord has anointed Me*
> *To preach good tidings to the poor;*
> *He has sent Me to heal the brokenhearted,*
> *To proclaim liberty to the captives,*
> *And the opening of the prison to those who are bound;*
> *To proclaim the acceptable year of the Lord,*
> *And the day of vengeance of our God;*
> *To comfort all who mourn,*
> *To console those who mourn in Zion,*
> *To give them beauty for ashes,*
> *The oil of joy for mourning,*
> *The garment of praise for the spirit of heaviness;*
> *That they may be called the trees of righteousness,*
> *The planting of the Lord, that He may be glorified."*
> *(Isaiah 61:1-3)*

As I re-read this passage, I am reminded of how much our Father and God is moved with compassion for the brokenhearted. It may not seem like it right now, but there is beauty in the ashes. You may be feeling disappointed and hopeless right now, and may be wondering, *When Lord? What about your promises?* Just know, there is beauty in the ashes of delay. There is beauty in the ashes of shattered dreams.

Today, just like God said to those ladies in that prayer room on that Saturday morning, He is speaking to your heart and calling you to step out of the season of brokenness. "Take off the ash covered grave clothes of yesterday's broken dreams and losses, and step into the new season of healing and refreshing I have for you. Today is a reawakening and a new beginning for all that I have for you."

As I left the prayer meeting that day, there was a sweet presence of the Lord surrounding me, and a settled place in my heart that marked the beginning of the best season of my life. It was confirmed by my dear friend and prayer partner, Nike who looked at me and said, "Shuronda, you will laugh again!" I looked at her with a thankful heart and nodded, "Amen!"

Mixing the Bitter and the Sweet

I had not spoken to my dear friend, Tedeen, in several months although I had been thinking about her a lot lately. So, I decided to give her a call. It was so wonderful to hear her cheery voice on the other end of the phone. After briefly exchanging pleasant hellos, she asked the probing question: "So, what's new and what's going on in your life?" I'm not sure I knew how to start, so I immediately asked her to tell me how she and her husband, Tom, were doing. It kept the focus off of me...if only temporarily.

As I began to share my heart about the place of brokenness I had recently walked through, and what seemed to be the shattering of my dreams with breaking off of the relationship I felt God had for me, I realized how tender it was still, to talk about. I was very encouraged as I talked to her, and I knew it was with a newfound place of trust in the Lord. Her words ministered to me like a refreshing well full of wisdom and understanding that only could have flowed from God. It was like she was answering questions that I had struggled with in my heart over the last few months. The biggest one being: *Why Lord? Why didn't it work out? He was great! I was great! And we both were very willing! Why did I have to walk through the pain of this?*

Tedeen shared the story of how she had taken the time to look up and study the meaning of her middle name, Marie, and the revelation God gave her. The inherent meaning of the name, Marie is *bitterness*. She shared how this had always bothered her that her name meant bitterness, until God began to teach her that in life there is a mixing of the bitter and sweet in our lives that brings about the fullness of what He truly desires for us.

Through her tremendous insight and powerful life testimony, God brought understanding to the purpose of the bitter crushing in my own life as I was reminded of the life of Jesus. You see Jesus faced His own crushing on the cross of Calvary for you and for me. You may not know that yet, but you can know it for yourself. Psalm 45 is a beautiful picture of our Messiah, Lord and King and the glorious wedding day between He and His bride, the church.

Read with me the verse found in Psalm 45:8.

*"All Your garments are scented with **myrrh** and aloes and cassia, Out of the ivory palaces, by which they have made You glad."*

Jesus was clothed with myrrh (which represents the sometimes bitter and harsh realities of life). It was one of the spices used in the preparation for his death. Just like

Chapter 3 ~ Standing at the Crossroads of Shattered Dreams

Jesus, the beauty of the anointing released in our lives, is made fragrant by mixing the bitter with sweet. We do not realize at the time, but it is sometimes the very ingredient of adversity and brokenness that brings out the full fragrance and power of the anointing in our lives. I call them "myrrh moments." It is what prepares and positions us in a greater way to fulfill the destiny God has for our life.

Myrrh Moments

Spend some time right now thinking about the "myrrh moments" in your own life. God always uses these moments in our life to produce the fragrance of who He is. We can exchange every "myrrh moment" for the sweet ointment of His anointing. It is a life-releasing fragrance (oil of gladness) that brings a healing aroma and sweet lingering fragrance and which produces an eternal, everlasting, deposit that remains...

Myrrh Moment	Sweet Lingering Fragrance
Example: Shattered dream of a broken relationship and deferred hope of marriage	*Example: Deeper vulnerability and greater capacity to love God and others*

Heavenly Father,

I get it and I'm getting it. You know all things and there is purpose in the crushing circumstances and events in my life, and from my past. I know that I do not have to stay in the pain of those things, and that I can rise victoriously out of the pile of ashes trading every myrrh moment for your sweet lingering fragrance into the beauty of the destiny You have for me.

At The Crossroads

As you can see, there are crossroads that we all come to in the pursuit of our dreams. And at the crossroads, there is always a choice. Will you move forward? Go back? Give up and continue to allow the ashes to bury your dreams? Exchange your ashes for the garland of beauty Jesus purchased for you. God wants you to know that you have a *pocketful of possibilities* as you walk with Him. What possibility will you choose today?

Chapter 4

Dreams That Live Again

"...I am going to put breath into you and make you live again!"
~ Ezekiel 37:5 (NLT)

*W*hatever happened to the American Dream? One day I was listening to an interesting internet news story. The host was interviewing a guest who was talking about *The American Dream*. Since I'm writing a book on realizing your dreams, my ears perked up, and I paused a few moments to listen in on his remarks. In his introduction, the commentator led in with the comment, *"The American Dream* use to be a home in the suburbs, a two car garage, with a backyard, picket fence, three kids and maybe a dog. The new American Dream is just having enough money to retire. He goes on to say that nearly fifty percent of the individuals polled said that their number one financial goal was having enough to retire. Only seventeen percent polled even considered the possibility of owning their own home with the current economic outlook."[1] For most folks, *the American Dream* had simply become one of "Survival." No more white picket fence, *survival is it.* There is no longer an aspiration to dream, it is just to survive. It is clear that there are enemies that have come in and eroded the idea of the American Dream.

Has merely survival become the dream that you accept for your life and for your family? Sadly, I find that many have settled into this place of existence rather than truly living out their dreams. Many choose daily to live in the valley of dream despair, allowing their dreams to be buried in a grave. That's not the dream I've accepted for myself or for my family. Jesus came that we might have life and to live it to the fullest (John 10:10). What about you? Are you ready to live the life God desires for you? Are you ready to uncover and recover your buried dreams?

The Valley of Dream Despair

I want you to think about it for a moment. Remember your dreams, your desires... your goals. Whatever happened to them? Are they filed away in a desk drawer? Are they stuffed on a shelf somewhere...collecting dust? It is time to take them down and blow the dust off. God wants to resurrect some dead dreams.

Chapter 4 ~ Dreams That Live Again

As I turned back to my thoughts, and the task at hand of writing my book, I flipped open my Bible and began to read Ezekiel 37. I had read this passage of scripture many times before but today it was different. The words were dancing on the page and quickly became the inspirational boost for my thoughts and creativity.

When I got to Ezekiel 37:11, I became very excited, because I saw it. I saw what the Lord was speaking to the children of Israel (who had gone into captivity in a foreign nation) about their dead and buried dreams. Dreams they had forfeited. Dreams that had been covered by the ashes of the sins and devastation of past generations! They had forgotten about the promise of God that He would return them to their homeland. They had relegated their hopes and dreams to just survival, sifting among the ruins and ashes.

Then God spoke to Ezekiel: "Son of man, these bones are the people of Israel. They say, 'Our bones are dried up and our hope is gone; we are cut off.'" (Ezekiel 37:11)

Their dreams were gone and they had accepted captivity as way of living. Even today, many have settled for their own captivity of fear or doubt...*this is all I've ever known*. The bondage of what's acceptable to others can sometimes be more comfortable than pursuing your dreams. Maybe no one else in your family has ever achieved anything great. Are you building your hopes and your dreams on the ashes of past generations, unable to soar in the dreams God has for you?

God longs to give you a future and a hope. God wants to restore hope. God wants to resurrect dreams from the valley of despair. God not only wants to resurrect dreams, He wants to heal the dreamer. He wants to bring healing to the brokenhearted and all the wounded places in your soul. He wants to restore your ability to dream and resurrect your faith to receive all that He has promised to you.

I have walked through many seasons in the valley of despair with hope that seemed long deferred on the dreams and the promises that God had spoken into my life. Then God spoke to those places of dry bones and the unbelief in my own life and said "Live, I am able to do all that I promised to you."

God desires for His people to take their dreams out of the wait because they are very much a part of the plan that He has in fulfilling their destiny.

"Yes, your destiny is unfolding, but you have to begin living in your dreams now. I am able to do what I say I will do in my Word. There is nothing too hard for Me, and there is nothing impossible. Believe Me. Believe that I am able to fulfill every dream because I have a pocketful of possibilities waiting for you to discover. I will return them; I will restore them; I will resurrect and bring back all that is lost. You can trust Me. I am Your Father and Your God!" (Prophetic expression)

Ezekiel spoke the same message to the children of Israel in chapter 37, verses 12-14. "Therefore prophesy and say to them: This is what the Sovereign Lord says: 'My people, I am going to open your graves and bring you up from them; I will bring you back to the land of Israel. Then you, my people, will know that I am the Lord, when I open your graves and bring you up from them. I will put my Spirit in you and you will live *(your dreams will live),* and I will settle you in your own land. Then you will know that I the Lord have spoken and I have done it, declares the Lord.'" Ezekiel 37:12-14 (NIV) *Emphasis added.*

There are many dreams buried in the graves of forgetfulness. You may think that all is lost. It isn't lost. God is bringing them up out of the graves today!

In receiving renewed hope for your dreams, you must answer three questions:

- Do I believe God is who He says He is?
- Do I believe He will do what He says He will do?
- Do I believe that He will do it for me?

Let's glean from the life of the Biblical character, Sarah. I have been reading about Sarah over the last few months and have looked at the things in her life that parallel my own. I'm not talking about her daily lifestyle, in comparison as a homemaker or business woman. I'm talking about the hopes and the desires she had for herself as a woman and for her family. Not only was her dream, a dream of becoming a mother, but her desire was to be productive and to produce the things God had placed within her. She is very much like you and me. We all long to be the best mothers we can be and to see produced in our lives the hopes and dreams God has spoken to us. Yet, when we first meet Abraham and Sarah in scripture, the first thing God says about them after the genealogy of their family intrigued me.

"Then Abram and Nahor took wives: the name of Abram's wife was Sarai, and the name of Nahor's wife, Milcah, the daughter of Haran the father of Milcah and the father of Iscar. But Sarai was barren, she had no child."
(Genesis 11:29, 30)

"But Sarai was barren and she had no child." I had to read it again. This was before God called them to do anything great. This was even before the promise. What I saw in Sarah's story (that encouraged me about my own hopes and dreams) is that God resurrects dead things, just as He spoke to the dry bones. So, if you are like me, waiting on the promise for a husband and a family of your own, even though you are way past forty; don't worry, God resurrects dead things...dead hopes, dead dreams and dead wombs! God chose Abram and Sarai on purpose to demonstrate there is nothing too hard for Him (Genesis 18:14).

I Will Return and Perform My Good Word to You

Sarah struggled to believe God. She had to answer the same questions we have to answer today. We know that she desperately wanted to believe God for the son He had promised her. She even thought that perhaps her hand-

Chapter 4 ~ Dreams That Live Again

maiden, Hagar, would be able to produce the son that she desired. *Yes, surely that would work.* Do you feel her desperation, her struggle, her conflict, and possibly now her hopelessness and resignation that it was too late for her? I know that many of you may feel this way. I did. I wondered, *Father, what about me?*

It's not that I didn't want to believe God. God is who He says He is, and I know that God is able to do what He says He will do. He will fulfill every promise He's made to you.

The book of Hebrews tells us in chapter 11, verse 11 that "By faith Sarah herself also received strength to conceive seed, and she bore a child when she was past the age, because she judged Him faithful who had promised."

During the time of writing this book, I walked through an incredible Bible study on believing God. The scripture reflection throughout this study strengthened and changed my life forever.

It came at a time in my life when my faith foundation was shaken, and I had begun to doubt many of the words God had spoken to me about the promises that He had for me.

But, when the throes of doubt and depression assailed my mind and my heart wanted to give up, the Lord would sing me a love song, *For You I Will.*

This is a song that is often played at weddings for doting couples as an expression of their love and affection for one another. I guess you could say that this was the same kind of expression God wanted me to understand in that moment, of His love for me.

His love flows so much deeper than mere words can even begin to convey. You see, *not only will God cross an ocean for you, He will bend heaven for you (Psalm 18:9).*
Not only will He give you the moon, He gave His very life for you (Matthew 20:8).

Through the echoing words and sweet melody of a song, God spoke faith to my heart about His promises for me. "Shuronda, I promise you, for you I will. I will visit you, and I will perform My good Word toward you. Don't give up; don't let your hopes dim."

God wants us to know the exceeding greatness of His power toward us. God spoke this to me because He loves me, and He desires to fulfill my dreams as He does yours.

"…I have loved you with an everlasting love; I have drawn you with loving-kindness." Jeremiah 31:3 (NIV)

God loves you right where you are this moment. Allow Him to speak to your storm today. Hear His whisper: "I promise you, for you I will." Whatever you need today, whatever dream you are holding onto, God's promise is that for you, He will do it.

Believing the God Who Speaks to Dead Wombs

Many of you may be saying, "What do you do when the answer doesn't come?" The years have come and gone and have turned to decades and still the promises are far off." Or you say, "It really is too late. How will God come through for me now?" It may be hard at times to believe God and to

Chapter 4 ~ Dreams That Live Again

receive the promises He has for you because of the many disappointments along the way. Maybe you have walked through years of frustration and seasons of delay wondering *did I hear God*. So, you resign yourself to the fact that maybe you just don't have enough faith or that it no longer matters at this point.

Maybe you have received those dream shattering words like my friend, Judy, who sat in her doctor's office (quietly praying), hoping for good news after her <u>third</u> round of fertility drugs. She and her husband, Karl, had had quite a journey over the last few years. They had stood, believing God for the promise of the child, Judy had seen in her dreams. She had stood on the word God had given her, and she believed God was going to do it. The news she received that day (after six years of trying to conceive) was devastating. "Mrs. Horton," her doctor said slowly, "the fertility results came back negative. Based on your test results, you will not be able to get pregnant."

Her heart sank, as she and her husband walked out of the doctor's office that day...the hope of promise was gone. The pain was unbearable as she got on the hospital elevator, only to take a short ride up to the next floor where she stepped out onto the hospital nursery floor to visit her sister who had just given birth (the real reason she had come to the hospital that day). She held that little child close in that moment, rejoicing with her sister. No one but she and her husband knew the sacrifice of her pain she could only offer to God.

As Judy walked through the next days, weeks and months, she found the courage to release her pain, disappointment, and her broken-heartedness to the Father, trusting somehow that in His Sovereignty, He would provide something better. But what about the dream and promise He had given her? Did she dare hope in spite of the doctor's report?

Year after year passed by, and her hopes turned to ashes of despair. Now over twelve years later, Judy had finally resigned herself to the fact that she and her husband would never have a child together. She was fine with that, but this particular day, it seemed that she saw pregnant women everywhere she went. *Okay God*, she thought, what *is this about?*

Over the last eighteen years, Judy had often felt like Hannah, having to continually face her own *Peninnah* every time she saw a pregnant woman or a nursing mother. How the taunts of the enemy assailed her mind. Discouraged, she thought...*What did I do wrong?* The crushing was unbearable, time and time again. But she had made her peace, so why would God allow it to be thrown in her face once again?

Then the thought came to mind that she should pick up a pregnancy test. *Now she just knew she was losing it*; but she felt a small nudge and prompting from the Lord. "Okay Lord, she said, if that is what you want me to do, fine. I don't know why I need it or what I'm going to do with it." Judy picked up the test and headed home to get ready for her husband who was returning from his business trip. She wanted to take extra care and get dressed to welcome him home.

Chapter 4 ~ Dreams That Live Again

As she walked into her bathroom, she was reminded of the pregnancy test. "Oh yes, let me complete this test." She had used hundreds of pregnancy tests over the years, so she didn't think this one would be any different. As she picked up the stick, to her stunned disbelief, it had registered positive. She couldn't believe it! She questioned...reasoning, "This has got to be a mistake." She couldn't believe the miracle unfolding right before her eyes.

What the Father revealed to Judy's heart in that moment is much like the word God spoke to me when I doubted the promises that He had for me as I continue to wait on the husband and children I have prayed about for many years. "Believe Me for all that I have for you; I am still the God who speaks to dead wombs."

God spoke to Judy's dead womb and her impossible dream was made possible. Today Judy (47) and her husband Karl (50) have a beautiful, healthy three year old son, Tyler for whom they give all glory to a God who doesn't forget His promises.

What my friend, Judy learned as she walked through the struggle of believing for God's promises, is this: God maintains His promise even when you give up hope. God keeps His promises. If He says He will do it, then He will. Everything in the kingdom of God works on God's timing. His promises do not come with an expiration date on them, so choose to believe Him today. His plans are far greater for you than you know, and the joy that comes when your dream is fulfilled is inexpressible (Proverbs 13:12).

Healing for the Brokenhearted Dreamer

In order for us to walk in the all-possibility-producing-faith, and to realize the fullness of our dreams, we must allow God to heal the dreamer in each of us. He wants to restore, resurrect and fully redeem every promise; every dream and even those you have yet to dream because they are buried deep within your broken heart. Remember the woman who wrote down on her piece of paper that she just wanted "to be able to dream." God desires to heal the dreamer in you.

I believe that broken-heartedness is one of the biggest obstacles to people realizing their dreams, and ultimately the fullest potential of their destiny. Earlier, I shared a staggering statistic as it relates to individuals achieving their goals. Only three percent of people ever achieve their goals. What about the other ninety-seven percent? This book is written to the ninety-seven percent, because I truly believe that God wants us all to realize the fullness of what He has for us.

As a counselor and a minister, I am sometimes asked, "Why doesn't this person just move forward? Healing is available to them, why don't they just receive it?" People don't receive healing not because it isn't something that they want. Many times, they simply don't know how to receive the healing that's available, and unfortunately, the church has been inadequate in responding to the needs of the wounded soul or simply the brokenhearted.

However, Jesus responds differently. He has compassion for the emotionally wounded and the hurting, whose need we sometimes struggle to relate to, because we often reject our own emotional neediness. Most of the time, we view neediness as a personal weakness and we will either deny it or strive to meet it in unhealthy ways.

Healing the brokenhearted soul doesn't just happen in a vacuum. Time *does not* heal all wounds as some of you may have heard. Even prayer alone will never do it. Healing occurs in the context of healthy relationships. Our first relationship is with God, then with ourselves, and finally with others.

We often discount the relationship with ourselves, and that is where a big part of the struggle comes in. Healing will only come as we learn how to process and release the pain of broken-heartedness resulting from unmet needs, unhealed hurts and unfulfilled expectations.

Missing Pieces

I remember a season early on in my journey when the pain was very real. One day, I was walking through the grocery store intent on picking up the items on my shopping list. As I rounded one of the aisles, I paused for a moment to look at several product brands on the shelf. Out of the corner of my eye, I noticed a woman standing beside me, just as intent it seemed, on finding the right product. We turned and looked at each other almost simultaneously, and I realized that the woman standing beside me was my Pastor's wife. We greeted and hugged one another, and then she looked at me and said, "I was praying for you and asked the Lord concerning healing for you. The Lord told me it is not something that was done to you, but it is something that wasn't done."

God revealed to me that day that it was something that was missing. It was the missing pieces in my soul...the unmet needs, unhealed hurts and unfulfilled expectations from my past that limited my ability to receive all God had for me. I realized that this was a divine encounter, and the "word" encouragement that I received that day brought insight and healing to the place of brokenness from which I was desperately struggling to find peace and deliverance. Little did I know that God would use this personal revelation in my life to set many spiritual and emotional captives free.

My dear Pastor Kathy may not know the depth of what she spoke as we casually walked together in the store that day, but I did. I remember her words from over twenty years ago as if they were spoken yesterday. She said, "God is going to take your weakness *(the place of your struggle)* and make it a strength *(a ministry that would impact others)*." (paraphrase of Hebrew 11:34b; italics added for emphasis)

Maybe you recognize that you have missing pieces (unmet needs or unhealed hurts from your own past) just as I did.

There may have been someone who didn't do something for you when they said that they would. Maybe it was your father, your mother, or some other family member that disappointed you when you were a child. This was my case. Growing up, there were times when I felt let down by my

Chapter 4 ~ Dreams That Live Again

dad. Over the years, I have encountered others who let me down, who broke their promises.

Broken promises result in unmet needs, unhealed hurts and unfulfilled expectations.

How does this affect the dreams we have for our lives?

We dream out of the capacity of our soul (our mind, our will, our emotions, our thoughts, our imagination). Missing pieces result in a broken heart, and more specifically, a broken soul. It is often the hidden places of the heart where these missing pieces bring the most pain and can limit your dreams. It could be the pain of rejection, abandonment, betrayal or watching your family go through a painful divorce. Divorce is not just a break-up of a husband and a wife. It causes emotional wounds, which affect all, including the children and other family members.

Yes, broken-heartedness happens because of things that are done (many times, devastating relationship losses, or very horrific and violently abusive things, which I have seen in counseling for many years now), and because of things that weren't done for you, which wound just as deeply.

Those things are the good things like love, acceptance, affirmation, affection, protection, and encouragement. God designed us so that these needs could only be met in the context of healthy relationships with one another.

Author, Liberty Savard, in her book, *Breaking the Power*, provides a simple but profound descriptive overview of unmet needs and unhealed hurts and how they affect us:

- Unmet needs are birthed when something good that should have happened in your life DIDN'T.
- Unhealed hurts are birthed when something bad that should not have happened in your life DID.
- Unresolved issues are birthed out of the ensuing anger and the confusion about WHY.[2]

Jesus came to heal the wounds from the things that were done to us and to heal the wounds resulting from when we didn't receive what we needed to feel the love, hope, and joy He desires for us.

"Jesus truly heals the broken in heart and binds up all their wounds" (Psalm 147:3)

Broken-heartedness can keep you from stepping into and fully realizing your dreams unless you allow God into the inward places of your heart. You can receive healing and wholeness to pursue *whole-heartedly* all of the unfolding possibilities to your life purpose, desires and dreams. God wants you to expect the best for your life.

What Happens When We Have Unmet Needs, Unhealed Hurts and Unfulfilled Expectations?

We build what I call "dream barriers." Dream barriers are simply belief structures or thought processes (a way of thinking) that block access to the creative power of God. Whatever you think, feel and believe about yourself will always expand or limit your dream capacity.

Wrong thoughts and beliefs about yourself will hold you back from the very things you want out of life. Whereas, positive and affirming thoughts move you in the direction of your dreams!

Getting to the root of the pain, need or confusion is necessary in order to receive healing and to begin walking in your dreams.

Your soul comprises your mind, will, thoughts, feeling and emotions, so we have to begin by dealing with each of these components and how they are affected by unmet needs, unhealed hurts and unfulfilled expectations.

Dealing with Your Unmet Needs, Unhealed Hurts and Unfulfilled Expectations

We must go to the source of our unfulfilled expectations and release it through forgiveness. Oftentimes, this will include God, yourself and others. Unfulfilled expectations of God, generally occurs when you have placed a time limit on the promise or promises He has for you.

For several years, each January, I believed that God would surely bring to pass the fulfillment of my deepest desire for a mate. I knew it would happen or desperately hoped it would happen each "new" year. And each December 31st, my hopes would be dashed to pieces.

Whether I realized it or not, I was disappointed and even angry with God. I had placed an expectation on God to perform something within my timeframe until I learned that the promise always come in His timing. I had to forgive and release God for not meeting my expectation. As a result, I released myself to truly believe God again for all He had for me.

You might be asking, unfulfilled expectations of *myself?* Yes, these are the places where you failed to measure up in your eyes, or so you might think. Maybe you have thought like I have that there is something else you need to do. Or, in your effort to bury the pain of your unfulfilled expectation, you settle... into what seems a more realistic, less than...expectation. Where is the expectancy in the God of all power and of all possibility?

This book is about possibility. God has always performed miracles. He gets excited when you believe Him for more. Miracles put a demand on His power...the power He longs to demonstrate for you. To meet every need, to heal every hurt, and to fulfill your greatest expectations.

To begin this powerful process of healing, I have listed a few steps below:

1. We must identify the unmet needs that have been buried under the ashes of denial. *(Examples of unmet relational needs include: acceptance, affection, affirmation, appreciation, attention, comfort, encouragement, respect, security, support, peace[3])*

    o Which of the relational needs go consistently unmet in your relationships?

    o What thoughts do you struggle with as it relates to the unmet needs in your life?

    o How does this make you feel?

    o How do you generally respond to the pain of unmet needs in your life?

2. We must forgive and release the unhealed hurts from our past. *(Who do you need to forgive and release?)*

3. We must confront and deal with the unfulfilled expectations of:
   - God
   - Yourself
   - Others (past and present relationships)

   List the unfulfilled expectations you have experienced in your relationships (past and present):

4. Finally, we must choose the new possibilities God has for us. What do you expect for yourself today?

Renewed Faith to Conceive and Release the Impossible

I have walked through dark places where God uncovered and revealed deep wounding in my spirit and my soul. Yet, He has brought His healing balm to mend and to bind up every hurt, wounded and broken place within. What I have found along the journey is that the Lord, the author and finisher of my faith, renews my strength and releases me to soar from one height to the next height as He unfolds His incredible possibilities for my life. He will do the same for you.

Chapter 4 ~ Dreams That Live Again

Prayer of Healing for the Brokenhearted Dreamer Within

Heavenly Father,

I recognize that there are a lot of wounded places buried deep within, many of them resulting from unmet needs and unhealed hurt from my childhood and past relationships. Lord, today, I bring the pain and discouragement of the unfulfilled expectations of all my hopes and dreams.

(Name your unfulfilled expectations here)

Your word says that You heal the brokenhearted and that you bind up every wound. Father, I ask that You would mend and comfort my broken heart right now. Lord, I confess and release to You now the feelings of despair, disappointment, fear, doubt, hopelessness...that would try to hold me back from realizing all You have for me.

Father, I choose to forgive those who have rejected and hurt me in the past, those who have broken their promises to me, those who have let me down.

(Name them here)

Father, I even forgive myself for the many mistakes I've made. Lord, I thank You that You forgive me. Your Word says that when I confess my faults and my sins and repent that You are just and faithful to forgive me and to cleanse me from all unrighteousness. So Lord, I thank You for doing that right now. I am forgiven. I am cleansed and made righteous.

Today, I receive Your joy and peace knowing that You have a glorious plan of unfolding possibilities for my life and my dreams. I thank You, Father that You are able to do miraculous things, redeeming all that is lost and bringing forth every promise. There is nothing too hard for you.

I give You praise and glory for You are faithful to Your Word and prophetic promises, and You are able to bring to pass all that You have spoken.

In Jesus Name I pray, Amen!

Chapter 5

Impossible Dreams Made Possible

"With men this is impossible, but with God all things are possible."

~ Matthew 19:26

When God gives us a dream, He doesn't tell us that we will oftentimes encounter tests and trials along the way to our dream fulfillment. I also find that God doesn't seem to be moved by the difficult circumstances or the seemingly insurmountable odds to our dream achievement. In fact, He chooses you because of it. Remember, God chose Abraham and Sarah and called them to produce a great nation even though Sarah was barren.

Angels in the Outfield

One of my favorite movies that I have enjoyed watching over the years is the 1994 classic, *Angels in the Outfield*. It is a charming and heartwarming remake of the 1951 film by the same name, and is produced by none other than Walt Disney.

This delightful movie is the uplifting story about a couple of young boys, Roger Bomman (played by Joseph Gordon-Levitt) and J.P. (played by Milton Davis, Jr.), who find themselves living in a foster home. They have experienced some of life's difficult circumstances. Roger's mother has passed away, and we are not told what happened to J.P.'s family. Roger still has limited visits from his father.

Roger has one dream...a dream for a family. He asks his dad when they'll be a family again. His father answers rather cynically and doubtfully, "When the Angels win the pennant" (speaking of the city's professional league baseball team).

Of course this sets Roger on the quest of seeing his favorite baseball team win the pennant (even though they are in last place in their division), an impossible feat. Roger offers up a prayer to God, asking for a little help so that he might realize his dream of having the family he desperately longs for. Much to his surprise, real angels show up and begin to help the team. To the amazement of the team's coach (played by Danny Glover), the fans and the community, the Angels go on to win the pennant (with just a little Divine and angelic intervention). In the end, Roger gets his dream family in a most unexpected way.

One of my favorite quotes from the movie is made by J.P. who wants to see the same angels his friend, Roger sees. It's the positive affirmation he makes throughout the movie: "It could happen!"[1] that should encourage us in our own dream pursuit.

It could happen!

My translation: "It is possible!" This movie is a fun reminder of faith and the power of believing God's Word.

The Bible tells us that there is nothing impossible for God (Luke 1:37). Actually, there is only one thing that is impossible for God. It is impossible for Him to lie (Heb 6:18). What dream has God imparted in your heart? What has He spoken to you about your life? It is possible!

What are YOU believing God for today? All things are possible to him who believes (Mark 9:23). Will you believe that He wants to do the impossible in your life?

Through the faith and the belief of one little boy in this movie, we see the impossible made possible. The dreams that you have for your life are possible through the God who made you and shaped you for the dreams He's called you to live.

A Beautiful Restoration Story

It was the culmination of life circumstances, weaknesses, many bad choices and a continual spiral downward that had brought my dad to the fate of this day. For more than twenty years, we had prayed, we had fasted and believed for God to bring forth healing and deliverance for him. Had God given up on him? It had been many years of heartbreak and disappointment and many in our family had given up hope.

It is painful to watch someone you love go down a path of destruction. Was this what my dad desired for himself? Maybe he had given up on himself...maybe he had given up on his dreams and on what God had for him.

I had prayed hundreds of times for my dad, "God deliver him; restore all that is lost." But today, I sat in the courtroom waiting for the judge's sentencing. "What about all of our prayers? Lord, what about all of the times I cried out for him and believed for great things to happen for him. You are a God of restoration. You have used me to bring restoration in the lives of many. What about my own family?" My dad was sentenced to two years in jail.

Although, I was sad for my dad and where he was in life, I was at complete peace. I knew in my heart that this was a brand new beginning for him, and deep down I knew that God wasn't done with him. It was August 1st, and as I thought about the date, I felt a gentle confirmation, as the number eight in scripture represents new beginnings.

God is faithful. Over the next two years, I watched a complete transformation in my dad; first a spiritual release, and then a heart transformation to one of joy and of excitement about life once again. God was renewing some things in my dad. I even grew in my relationship with him like never before...something I had always desired since I was a little girl. To my surprise, my dad even wrote me letters sharing more of who he was, and I began to get to know him

Chapter 4 ~ Dreams That Live Again

better. God had a plan all along and I realized that He had preserved and kept my dad for now. This was a miracle indeed, as I know that there were many times when his life could have been cut off. But, God was faithful to my dad and to me. He fulfilled one of the deepest desires and prayers of my heart (setting my dad free) that only He knew.

I began this book by sharing about the restoration in my own life of my broken hopes and dreams and how redeeming, how thorough, how complete God's restoration and deliverance truly is. Likewise, for my dad, I saw God's complete restoration and the redemption of seemingly discarded dreams and failed hopes. The God of "impossible dreams, made possible" transformed my dad's life into something of beauty.

From the ashes of devastation to one gloriously set free!

Today, our family celebrates a man made whole, a son delivered, a father returned, and a grandfather revealed. My dad is very grateful for all of the great things God has done in his life as evidenced in how he lives today.

From the ashes of devastation, brokenness and addiction to one gloriously set free to be used by God for a great Kingdom work. He has made such a powerful impact in my brothers' lives and in my own, through the love and support of his family. He has also influenced and encouraged other men who have walked through similar life challenges, through his church's Celebrate Recovery Bible study group.

I am very proud to call my dad my friend, and I love him for the man he is and the man he is becoming. I tell my dad all the time...although he is now semi-retired, "God is not done with you yet. You have to share your testimony with others."

God will do for you what He did for my dad. My dad stepped into the gloriously new and unfolding possibilities that God had for him. Possibilities he thought were lost. You can too!

There is nothing too hard for God!

As with my life, with my dad's and others, you'll see that there is nothing too hard for God. He is the God of the impossible. He wants to release you to live your dreams.

So go for it! It's time to walk in the incredible possibilities that God has for you! It's time to take your dreams out of the wait!

Chapter 6

Taking Your Dream Out of the Wait

"Your dreams grow when put into action."

Many of you may have seen the 2006 movie, "Last Holiday." If you haven't, this would be a great movie to rent. Actress, Queen Latifah plays a young woman, Georgia Byrd, who has all these dreams that she puts in a "Possibilities" book.

Not until she reaches a place where she doesn't have anything to lose does she actually take steps toward fulfilling her dreams. She begins with one thing that she has always longed to do, which is visit the "Grand Pupp Hotel" in Switzerland. As she takes this step, she encounters connections along the way that opens the door for more of the opportunities and possibilities she has always longed to experience. She meets Chef Didian, who becomes a catalyst and partner in helping her to realize and fulfill her dream of becoming a chef and opening her own restaurant. She emerges as a confident and influential woman who impacts others along the way as she steps into all of her dreams.

Through these new experiences, she discovers a newfound freedom and adventure, and realizes how much of her life had been lived in the shadows of fear. Each step she takes conquers the fear in her heart, and her reality expands into the never imagined dreams she has always desired. Actually, they were imagined in her book of Possibilities. This movie is a great reminder for each of us.

Envisioning what can be is our first step. We must begin to see all of the possibilities that God has for our lives. His Word tells us that He knows the thoughts (possibilities) that He has for us, thoughts (possibilities) to prosper us and not to harm us, to give us a future and a hope in our expected outcome in life. God has shaped so many incredible possibilities that He is just waiting to unfold along life's pathway.

What did Georgia have to overcome? She had to overcome her fear and confront what she believed about herself. She didn't have a problem with dreaming. Remember, she had this huge book of possibilities. She had a problem with believing that the dreams were for her, and that they were for her, now. Because she was afraid, she had a problem with taking the steps necessary toward the fulfillment of her dreams. Remember, God gives us dreams, not just for dreaming, but for fulfilling.

It Really Is Up to You

Enough is enough! It was 2:00 a.m. and it was another sleepless night. I had reached the point of complete frustration once again. I was frustrated with myself, frustrated with where I was, frustrated with my yet unrealized dreams and desires, and I was venting to the Lord. I was really trying to work through the disappointing emotions I was feeling about my career and ministry, when I suddenly stopped praying. The thought came to my mind: *It really is up to you!*

I got up and decided, *I'm going to own my dream. It's my dream so what am I going to do about it?* I realized that the same energy that I was expending being frustrated about my unfulfilled dreams, I could put into actionable steps toward achieving my dreams. These actionable steps are the goals that bring your dream into fulfillment.

There are times when a deep disappointment can cause you to get stuck in a place of frustration.

Frustration is defined as a feeling of disappointment, exasperation, or weariness caused by goals being thwarted or desires unsatisfied.

Many times we stay frustrated because it is easier to blame someone else, God perhaps, because He hasn't done what He said He would do. I have been there, but learned many years ago that BLAME comes down to: ***B**elieving **L**ies **A**nd **M**aking **E**xcuses.*

A Pocketful of Possibilities

The more real we become with ourselves, in understanding how we relate to life around us, then the more empowered we become to see our dreams come to pass. Honestly, ask yourself and God the following questions.

- What emotions challenge me on a daily basis?

- What lies do I believe about my dreams, my desires, and my circumstances?

- What excuses, decisions and/or lack of decisions have I made that keep me from realizing my dreams?

- What am I willing to do about it now that I know?

After answering these questions for myself, I determined that I wouldn't spend one more sleepless night, frustrated. I have decided to spend that time creating, writing books, developing new coaching curriculums or a spiritual warfare series.

Often confused with the word frustration, discontentment is different. It is defined as dissatisfaction or a longing for better things; a restless desire for something better.

I believe God places discontentment in us for a reason. Many times, He wants us to see that it is time to move into action. It is time to:

- Move on from that relationship that isn't going anywhere.
- Move on from that dead-end job...develop a plan, establish some goals and steps to transition, but move on.
- Move toward the great things that God has for you. It really is up to you!

Sometimes, people get stuck and stay in one place for years. You may feel your dream has died, and that you can't move on. It may be that you really don't know how to move forward. You are stuck in the pile of ashes of whatever...you fill in the blank.

Get beyond your disappointment and move on. Develop a time limit and just do it. It's time to move on. It's time to step onto your stage of possibility.

Step Onto the Stage of Possibility

This morning wasn't unlike any other morning. Although, I was intent on sleeping a little longer than usual or at least until 9 a.m., I was suddenly interrupted by the ringing of my cell phone. I said "No, I'm sleeping to 9 a.m." but it was too late. I knew I had a meeting I planned to attend in a couple of short hours, so why not get a jump on it. I mulled around for a few minutes as I usually did when waking up, and then suddenly I realized, I better get going if I'm going to make it to my scheduled meeting. It was a small group meeting hosted by one of the ladies from my church. I was excited to attend as I had heard a lot about her meetings, and knew the impact she was making. I also wanted to support and encourage her in what she was doing. Although, I went to encourage and support her, I found I was encouraged the most. It's quite amazing to see how God will use new events and connections to inspire and move you toward the things He has for you...to push you a little bit.

I am actually known for pushing others a little bit, as I am passionate about putting a demand on the greatness I see in them. As a coach and a consultant, I live to draw out the gifts and talents in others and to help position them for their God-ordained success.

The group leader spent some time talking about how to begin shifting your perspective as it relates to seasons of transition in your career. She invited the women to share where they were in their career transitions. There were several women present who had come for various reasons: some who had been launched into a time of transition as a result of a company downsizing; some who were taking a leap of faith in starting their own business; and some who were working, but knew there was something more for them. Most of all, those who were present were looking for what to do next.

I was excited to hear as the ladies shared from their experiences and where they were. Jo, one of the ladies who attended regularly, shared a comment that made me think about where I was in my own life, and really where I am in what I have called a *long transitional season*. Let's admit it, we're all in some place of transition, and by the end of this book, I want to show you how great times like these can be. Seasons of transition can be a catalyst, which propels you toward the realization of your goals and life dreams whether in your career, home, ministry, or relationships.

As Jo shared with the group, she posed the question, "Are you sitting in the boat or are you walking on the water?" The *pocketful of possibilities* God has for us will almost always require us to get out of the boat and walk. We have to begin walking toward our dreams if we ever intend to see them realized. Many of us have an "in the box" or should I say "in the boat" mentality, and we don't ever venture out to do the unexpected or even consider the impossible.

It's time to step onto the stage of possibility. God wants to expand your perspectives to begin to see creatively and innovatively. He wants to show you how to live the life He's designed for you, and that you've always desired. Let's stop just dreaming and let's start living it.

Dream Positioning

I always coach individuals to do something even if it is a small thing. Several years ago, I felt God stirring my heart toward a new venture. I wasn't quite sure what to do. I had been in a time of transition, a season where God had moved me from all that I knew and depended upon. Let me share my journey. I can recall it like it was yesterday. During this time, I could sense very strongly God's leading and direction.

I had been asked if I would consider taking a position on staff at my church to work with our pastors over Singles Ministry. I knew God had His hand upon my life and that He had called me to full-time ministry. I also knew the anointing that He had placed on my life, and the specific way I felt my spiritual gifts would be used. So I wasn't sure about the Singles Ministry role; it didn't quite line up with what I believed was the ministry call. No matter what it looked like, I still knew in my heart and felt this was God's direction, and that He was opening the pathway for this new opportunity.

I accepted the position and prepared my resignation letter for my manager and the company for whom I worked. Because I was a corporate trainer and had several workshops scheduled over the next couple of months, I felt it was my duty to provide as much notice as possible so the company could plan and staff for my job role. At the time, I was the only trainer for my product and service area. I confidently submitted my resignation letter giving them a six-week notice. I had discussed this with the pastors at my church and they had agreed, even though their current staff assistant had given notice and would be leaving on Friday, May 1st. They wanted me to begin right away, but I really didn't see how I would be able to do it without leaving my company in a bind. I felt I needed to give as much notice as possible. I was motivated by the fact that this was the right thing to do and it was. But, was this my complete motivation? A couple of days after giving my manager my resignation letter, God began speaking to my heart about the timeframe I had established with "my" transition plan. He said, "May 1st is your last day." I said, "But Lord, I can't go back to my manager and tell him that I have to change my leave date of May 15th to May 1st. How is that going to look?" I think I was more concerned with how I would I look. He said "Okay, you can stay until the extended notice date you gave, but the grace is up on May 1st." I quickly said "Okay, Lord." I'd much rather be within a place of His grace and covering than outside of it. Many times in seasons of transition, we stay too long and suffer far too much rather than taking a step of faith toward all that God has for us.

As I prayed and talked to the Lord more, He revealed that my motivation for giving a six-week notice was rooted in fear. I was about to leave my cushy corporate job and take a huge pay cut to take this position in my church. I was single and the sole provider of my household. I secretly wondered, "Would the Lord take care of all my needs?" I was going to have to trust Him in a whole new way. God elevated my understanding of who He was, as He led me down this new path of possibility, moving me progressively toward the dreams and greater fulfillment of the purpose and destiny He has for me.

It gets better. I went back to my manager, and told him that I needed to adjust my last day to May 1st. Over the following weeks as I finished out my assignment, I had the opportunity to celebrate with my fellow employees at a big, going away party with lots of fun sharing after ten years of employment. I also received my last paycheck inclusive of my vacation time and a surprise final installment of a bonus that I was only entitled to if I was still working with the company on May 1st. I had completely forgotten about the bonus. What a God we serve! He has complete control of every detail in our lives. He didn't forget about the bonus that He had for me, and He allowed me to stay until all that I had coming...came to me.

We can always trust God for the unfolding plan He has for us. His plan is to prosper us and not to harm us, to give us a future and a hope. And more importantly, He wants us to realize every dream and desire that He has given us. The fulfillment of every dream is a part of the grand design of the destiny and purpose He has called us to. It is time to start living your dreams today. Discover all of the possibilities that God has created to get you there!

Let's fast-forward a few years of working on staff in ministry. I began to feel a familiar stirring in my heart that seemed to imply my season was changing. Did God have something else for me to do? I was passionate about my ministry role and what I was doing. But, after years of serving in this capacity, I was struggling with burnout. I was longing to stretch my gifts in a new way. What new possibilities did God have for me next?

Creating Your Roadmap of Possibilities

Uncovering all of the possibilities God has for your life requires you to do something. I'm sure you have heard the statement that *it's easier to steer and direct a moving car rather than a parked or stalled one.* I'm not sure who originated this quote, but I do know that God originated its thought.

His word declares in Psalm 37:23, "The steps of a good man are ordered by the Lord and He delights in his way." One of the key words found in this scripture is "steps." The word itself denotes action as its definition bears out. It means: *short movements with your feet; a way of walking, and my favorite, a stage in a progression toward some goal or target.*

God has this incredible plan with many possibilities (potential and promises) yet to be discovered as you walk out your destiny. The problem is that God can't order your life and all of its opportunities for growth and fulfillment of your dreams if you are not stepping forward. One of the things that I find most meaningful in this scripture is the delight God receives in you taking steps, and your way of walking out all He has for you. With every step, you are positioning yourself for the success God has for you.

One of the *4P Success Strategies* that I developed and now use in my coaching business is the principle of "Positioning."

Positioning ~ "Taking steps big or small...building the framework for the realization of your goals"

I still remember sitting down with my friend, Stephanie, and talking about where I was and what I wanted to do next. If you do not have someone that provides a collaborative voice in your life, then find one. In the years that I have known her, she has been that voice of reason, always encouraging, always provoking me to thought, always taking what I'd like to do and adding a creative presentation to it. Let me just ask you, have you ever been around people who have this unique ability to say something in a way that creatively flows? And you wonder *how did they come up with that?* That's my friend, Stephanie. She is the collaborative catalyst behind the *4P Success Strategies.* She took the heart of what I desired to convey in my coaching and training and helped shaped them into principles that I teach and articulate now in all I do.

It comes back to that day of taking one small step to move forward in the direction God had for me. Did I have it all figured out? Absolutely not, and even now, I can say that I'm still *taking steps big and small, building the framework for the realization of my goals.* The thing is, that as I build the framework, I get a bigger glimpse of the picture that God is unveiling. It's looking pretty good!

What keeps you from taking that step, whether it is starting your business, transitioning into a new career, stepping out there in your own ministry, or pursuing other goals and dreams? I hear you now...yes, for most it is fear.

We are all challenged with fear and it is something that we will deal with as we move forward in this book. I want to discuss a bigger challenge that I believe is closely tied to fear. Most of you will agree that once you have tried something, your apprehension...your fear, if you will, is removed. It was that way for my mom.

Many years ago, my mom had never flown on an airplane. Although an adult, she had never flown and was quite afraid of flying. Well, I wanted to bless my mom by taking her on a vacation of a lifetime to Hawaii. Yes, an eight hour flight to Hawaii would be her first airplane trip. She did great and is still living and breathing as she shares. That one experience empowered my mom to move beyond and break her fear of flying. She has since flown to other places because she stepped out there to fly once. She empowered herself by taking a step.

The biggest challenge that keeps many from stepping into and realizing their dreams is that they are waiting for others to empower them. One of my favorite authors, Dondi Scumaci, says in her book, *Designed for Success*:

"Empower yourself, what are you waiting on."[1]

In order to release the *pocketful of possibilities* for your life, you will have to look for ways to empower yourself. What do I mean? Do you consider yourself assertive? Or are you willing to go after what you want?

To empower means *to authorize, to give authority or power to*. 2 Timothy 1:7 says that God has not given you a spirit of fear, but of love, of power and of a sound mind. So rather than focusing on fear, let's focus on something that will release your ability to be successful in accomplishing your dreams and your goals.

The Strong Concordance Greek reference for *power* is *dynamis (G1411)*.[2] The power of God in this scripture actually refers to strength, power and ability. It is closely related to possible as in the scripture reference:

"...all things are possible to him who believes." The Greek reference for *possible* is *dynatos (G1415)*.[3] I find it interesting that the same power that removes our fear is the same power that produces our possibilities.

Sometimes, empowering yourself is simply giving yourself permission. Permission to agree with God about what He has said about you, about what He desires for you and about what you desire for yourself. When I begin the coaching process with new individuals, a couple of the questions that I always ask them include:

1. What do you expect for yourself?

2. What possibilities do you want to add to yourself?

They are very similar questions, yet different. My goal is to help individuals think about options they have never considered. In other words, if you were dreaming, what are some of the possibilities that you desire, or really what are some of the things that you think are impossible where it requires God's power to makes possible?

Back to the business mentor group meeting I attended. One of the ladies shared that with her recent transition from her job, she was now at a point of really thinking about what she'd like to do. And then she said something which reminded me of this very thing of dream positioning. She said that she had considered a new career path in technology or education (two areas she was most passionate about), but with the current economy, she wasn't sure.

Individuals often believe they only have option A or option B and do not recognize that option C or D are possibilities to explore. They limit the possibilities that they believe God desires to bring in their life. I immediately responded posing the question if she had considered developing her own training program that bridges her passion of education and helping others in technology, to which she responded no. It was a light bulb moment that made her think "outside of the boat." Oftentimes, it is hard to see the possibilities and opportunities right before you. Yes, it is often hard work, and seemingly impossible, but it is so worth it when you step into your dream. I have found that in the midst of explored possibilities, purpose is discovered.

Recognizing Purpose in Every Opportunity

Discovering purpose is probably one of the hardest things I see individuals struggle with. They long desperately to do the will of God. They want to be used by Him. But oftentimes, their God given assignment and purpose eludes them. In Jeremiah 29:10-14, we can believe and agree that God has a plan for us and that it is a plan for good, for prosperity, and we can all use a little more of that, right. Financially, spiritually and physically speaking! We want to be at our best and have the best that God has for us. But many are asking the question, what is that plan? What is my purpose? What is my assignment? Often, we have made finding our purpose much harder than I believe God intended. In Jeremiah 29, verse 14 tells us that we will find Him when we search for Him with all of our hearts.

I remember a teaching by my pastor introduced many years ago on *Discovering the Shape of Your Ministry*. He taught some key insights and very practical principles on how to find your purpose through the recognition of your unique design and the experiences that have shaped you.

This concept of the *Shape of Your Ministry* was developed by Erik Rees, pastor and author of the book *S.H.A.P.E.: Finding & Fulfilling Your Unique Purpose for Your Life*. He has helped to empower thousands for Kingdom purpose through his revelatory teaching. In his book, he shares how your assignment can be recognized by:

1. Your **S**piritual gifts – What gifts do you have?
2. Your **H**eart's desires – What do you like to do? What are you most passionate about? What excites you? What are you drawn to?
3. Your **A**bilities – What are your natural aptitudes, talents or abilities?
4. Your **P**ersonality – How do you express life?
5. Your **E**xperiences – What have you walked through? What are your testimony, background, and experiences?[4]

This revelatory teaching changed my life. For many years now, I have used these keys to direct me in my own assignments, trusting the God who fearfully and wonderfully made me and uniquely designed me for His purpose. The responsibility that He has given me is developing these areas so that I realize and walk in more of the purpose that He has called me to. You can too. You can go from one height to the next height, discovering the unfolding possibilities in your purpose. Assignments may change as we grow, but our purpose remains the same...seeking and finding more of God through the discovery of who we are in Him. Hallelujah! Aren't you glad we have a pocketful of possibilities in Him!

The Path Isn't Always Clear But Unfolding

One of the biggest challenges during this economically hard season is the number of individuals losing their jobs. Whether it is a result of the corporate downsizing or the taking of that next step in a new season, it can be hard to creatively see the opportunity in the transition. When praying for and coaching individuals who have been laid off, I encourage them by shifting their perspective away from the negative viewpoint. I share with them that this isn't a layoff; this is a launch and an opportunity to step into something brand new and to expand their horizon. I ask the question, what possibilities would you like to add to your life right now?

Seeing My Path Unfold

I remember the transition from my staff ministry job to starting my own business and ministry. I knew transition was coming. I had been feeling it for sometime over the last few years. I had actually taken a few steps by transitioning into various new job roles in the organization in which I worked. However, I still didn't feel prepared when transition came. It wasn't a transition I chose, although I knew it was God. As in the case with organizational changes and corporate downsizing, you find yourself feeling a little out of control and at a loss for what to do next. The timing was scary, especially with the many uncertainties in the economy. I remember how my pastor, who is a great mentor and friend, encouraged me to see that this was an opportunity to be launched into the greater things that God had for me. She knew how structured I was; and shared that this would be an opportunity for me to step out of the box, and expand my gifts and my talents. Boy was she right! God had been preparing it for me all along. He had spoken a prophetic word to me a few years before saying that *it was time; that He was pushing me out of the nest and it was time for me to fly!* It was seven years to the day, and a reminder that God had brought completion to this specific assignment and was providing a new one...an expanding one! My ministry call and purpose didn't change. It was an elevation to the next assignment and a release to the fulfillment of my dreams in a greater way. This transition became my launching pad out of the nest into the broad open wonder of flying. I've been flying ever since! If you find yourself walking through a transitional season, just remember: Stop groping around in the nest. It is time for you to fly!

Book of Possibilities

As we began this chapter, Georgia Byrd showed us that sometimes you have to take a big step. Other times, it is simply taking one small step at a time. God also reveals in

His Book, in Psalms 139:16-18, the magnitude of the possibilities that He has for us to walk in every day.

> *"Your eyes saw my substance being yet unformed.*
> *And in Your book they all were written.*
> *The days fashioned for me*
> *when as yet there were none of them.*
> *How precious also are your thoughts to me, O God!*
> *How great is the sum of them!"*

As I pondered this scripture one morning during my quiet time, God whispered to my heart, "Did you know that I have a "Book of Possibilities" for you?" My imagination began to explode with all the potential possibilities that God might have for me in this one day. As I meditated on it more, I realized that I could step forward to create them. Yes, God designed you for incredible, manifold possibilities. He's been "Imagineering" them all along. Will you step into them?

What is it that begins to move us toward our dreams?

1. **Begin to envision the possibilities** – Envision means to imagine, to foresee, to see, to visualize, to picture, to predict. Seeing it in the natural will help you move in the direction of your goals. How do you do this? Create a vision board of where you want to go. God even tells us to write the vision and make it plain so that he who read it

may run with it (Hab 2:3). We begin living our dreams by first envisioning it.

2. **Establish your possibilities network** – Partnering with others, friends, mentors, or life coaches, is a huge key to achieving your goals and dreams. My collaboration with my friend, Stephanie was an invaluable support and motivation toward me finishing and publishing my first book. If you need help, visit the ***myPossibility*** link at **www.walkinginpossibility.com** to connect with other women who share your passion.

3. **Enjoy the unfolding journey** – Your pathway to greatness and your personal success is not just a destination. The entire process is a rich part of the journey. Remember, Joseph and the dream he had. The dream wasn't merely about his brothers bowing down to him. The purposeful backdrop was much bigger. God had called Joseph to greatness. His dream, just like our dreams, was the vision seed or focal point that directed him and kept him moving. It was a part of the unfolding thoughts and plan God had for him. The thing is...he had opportunities and possibilities that he discovered along the way.

Envisioning the Possibilities

What steps did I take? I took a white cardstock poster board, my dreaming canvas, and a handful of magazines I used to capture the thoughts of God, and what He had laid out for me in words and pictures. As a result, my vision board now hangs on the wall in my office, encouraging me in each step that I take toward the unfolding possibilities that God has mapped out for my life. I am proud to say that it includes a picture of the bestselling books, I will write someday. I stand in awe as I see them come to pass. It began with me envisioning the things I wanted to add to my life.

What about you? What possibilities would you like to add to your life? There is nothing too big, so fill up your list. Remember you have pocketfuls....keep pulling them out and fill your field with the sunflowers of God as you journey on your way.

Take Your Dream Out of the Wait, Today!

When I first began writing this book, I had no idea where it would end up. Today it is in your hands. Whatever the dream, I do know that you have to get started by living it today. As you follow your heart, you will step into the amazing, unfolding possibilities designed for you, and discover that with God, the impossible really is made possible.

> *"Go confidently in the direction*
> *of your dreams!*
> *Live the life you've imagined."*
> *Henry David Thoreau*

Conclusion

Your Dream Made Possible

"When dreams come true, there is life and joy."
~ *Proverbs 13:12*

I sat in the coffee shop today with my friend, Karla. Her picture is the one that graces the cover of the very book you hold in your hands. I was excited to give her one of the new promotion cards introducing the book. It's amazing how many people recognized her, and called her about her part in the release of my very book. When others asked Karla how she came to be on my book cover, she shared that she thought it was because she was my first client. I hadn't realized the significance until that very moment.

A Pocketful of Possibilities

You see, I had totally forgotten that Karla was my very first business and coaching client. It was several years ago that this beautiful woman, with this huge vision, called me and said "I know you don't know me very well, but I feel like I need to connect with you. I'm launching a ministry, and feel like you are to be involved...maybe as a part of the Board of Directors." Although I told her that I would not be able to be a part of her ministry Board, I shared with her that her call was indeed orchestrated by God, and that maybe I could help her in another way.

As she spoke to me about her vision for her ministry and business, my heart began to overflow with excitement, and I knew God was using her to confirm my next step toward launching my own coaching and consulting business. When considering starting my business, I had prayed, "Lord, send the right individuals and businesses to me. Let them seek me out and call me. You know what I have to offer to them. I want to be a blessing to those you send to me." God hears our prayers and He never fails to produce His word in our lives. This divine connection and partnership over many years helped release the rich possibilities that I now walk in today. I took that small step toward my dream fulfillment, and not only did God unfold a *pocketful of possibilities* in my life, He used me to unfold the same in Karla's and many others along the way. That's the message of this book...the discovery of His possibilities and your dreams made possible.

Full Circle

Sitting there in the coffee shop, I was overwhelmed with gratitude at the recognition of God's hand upon me, and His intricate involvement in every detail of my life, even down to the design of my book cover. I am so moved even as I write this story. In fact, my book was ready to go to print and I had to rush home and write this excerpt. I just couldn't leave it out. The vision of the book cover and Karla's contribution was too important.

When the designer of the book cover said that she couldn't find the right photo, I immediately called Karla and asked if she would be willing to pose for the shot. She quickly and willingly agreed even before I had provided all the details. Thank you, Karla!

Well, we thought perhaps the graphic artist would use her more in the background, and that she probably wouldn't be recognized. But God is in the details, and was orchestrating something special for both Karla and me. He brought our paths full circle and revealed His thumbprint upon the *pocketful of possibilities* along our journey.

He also did something even more special for me. He confirmed for me that this was the final piece to this book and that now, it was ready. What an amazing God we serve!

Significance in the Details

I wanted my book cover to look like a Disney movie poster. Walt Disney has produced some of the greatest family movies inspiring all of us to dream. So, I wanted the inspiration of dreams made possible to shine through. On the cover, my dear friend, Karla represents the many women, who may have found themselves, standing at a crossroads of shattered dreams. But, when we realize that we are a huge part of creating our own roadmap of possibilities (represented by the plentiful sunflowers that we pull out of our pockets everyday), our dreams began to soar (as seen in the lift of the cloud-encircled, colorful balloons). And what was once barren land of ash covered and buried dreams, now becomes a field brimming with dancing sunflowers. God truly gives beauty for ashes and turns your sorrows into joy.

As we conclude our journey together, I pray you will continue to discover the unfolding and limitless possibilities God has written for your life. You'll find that with God all things are possible, and as you get out of the boat and walk, your dream is made reality.

Dream Journey Testimonial

I wanted to share with you a few of the dreams of my sisters who have inspired me during the writing of this book, and a very special dream journey testimonial. As I said earlier, this book is not just about the dream examples written herein, but it is about the realization of YOUR dreams. At the end I have included dream journey note pages for you to write your hopes, dreams and desires. Remember, that "writing your vision and dream" is the first step to fulfilling it (Habakkuk 2:3).

Pile of Dreams

"My Very Dream Realized"
by Tami Chalhoub

The women's conference at my church was coming up and I had such a sense of expectancy. I even took a day off from work to attend...believing that if I showed up, God would have something special for me. One of the sessions I attended that day was "A Pocketful of Possibilities" with speaker, Shuronda Scott. It was all about dreaming. She challenged us to recall the dreams we'd put on hold, and to pull them off the shelf, dust them off, and begin to activate them.

Women all around me were so moved. I saw tears flowing as women began to dig deep to uncover their dreams.

Yet, I sat still. At the end of the session, we were asked to write down our dreams to be placed in a dream box. Pen in hand, I struggled to think of a dream. It had been so long since I had allowed myself to imagine anything big. I couldn't think of a single dream. I decided to keep it simple. For many years prior to the conference, I had prayed that God would allow me to somehow use my gifts and expertise that I had built in the corporate arena in ministry. I wasn't quite sure what that would look like, and after awhile when it didn't happen, I stopped praying about it. But sitting there in that moment, that desire floated up and I quickly wrote it down on a piece of paper. I closed my eyes, prayed and put my dream in the dream box.

Well a few months after the conference, I attended a Women's Power Luncheon for business owners and professional women in my church. I'm a bit of an introvert, and normally do not like to attend events like this on my own. But, I decided not to let that stop me. As it turned out, Shuronda Scott was also the host of the luncheon. When it was over, there was a line of women waiting to talk with her. I wanted to approach her as well, but I am certainly not that type of person either! After rehearsing a few minutes in my head what I was going to say, I walked up to her and introduced myself. What a divine connection that turned out to be!

I learned that our Women's Ministry was in the initial stages of creating a mentoring program for women in business. In my career as a Human Resources professional, I have mentored countless people, and even led mentoring and development programs. This was the opportunity I had been praying for! Before I knew it, we were launching the ministry and I was one of the leaders. It has been a tremendous blessing. I can honestly say that I have truly gained more than I have given.

Wasn't that just what I had prayed for all of those years? I had given up on that dream, and forgotten about it, but God had not. Two years later, I had the opportunity to host an event at our church for women in business, and Shuronda was our keynote speaker. As I looked out at over a room full of women, while holding the microphone, ready to speak, I began to cry. I realized that this was the very same room where I had written down my dream and, placed it in the dream box. I was moved and overcome by what God had done in such a short period of time. Just two years ago, I struggled to think of a single dream, and now a long forgotten dream has been realized.

I'm enjoying and thriving in this new ministry role, and I know that God is not done. This is only the beginning. He wants me to continue to dream. The amazing thing is...His dreams for us are even bigger than we can possibly imagine. So don't be afraid to let your dreams run wild, and know that the Creator of the universe wants nothing more than to give you the desires of your heart.

I want to thank you Tami for sharing your dream journey testimony with us. You are an amazing woman and a gifted writer! I can't wait to see all the dream fulfillment of the other desires of your heart.

Just as Tami discovered, our God is faithful to produce in our lives all the seeds that have been planted.

*Keep dreaming
One dream pushes open the door for the next and expands your possibilities and destiny!*

Notes

Chapter 1: Pile of Dreams
1. Walt: The Man Behind the Myth (Documentary produced by Walter Elias Disney Miller, Released 2001).
2. Dondi Scumaci, *Ready, Set...Grow!* (Lake Mary, FL: Excel Books, 2009).

Chapter 2: God's Plans for Your Dreams
1. The New Open Bible Study Edition, The New King James Version (Nashville, TN: Thomas Nelson, 1982).
2. http://en.wikipedia.org/wiki/Walt_Disney_Imagineering, Retrieved 2012-03-26.
3. http://en.wikipedia.org/wiki/Imagineering, Retrieved 2012-03-26.

Chapter 3: Standing at the Crossroads of Shattered Dreams
1. Dondi Scumaci, *Ready, Set...Grow!* (Lake Mary, FL: Excel Books, 2009).
2. http://www.merriam-webster.com/thesaurus/ashes, 2012-03-26.
3. Song written by Mary Alessi, *I Will Bless the Lord* (Pressing On Album, © 2009, Miami Life Sounds Publishing INC. BMI)

Chapter 4: Dreams that Live Again
1. http://www.mainstreet.com/article/retirement/new-american-dream-retirement, Retrieved 2012-03-28.
2. Liberty Savard, *Breaking the Power* (North Brunswick, NJ: Bridge-Logos, 1997).

3. David and Teresa Ferguson; Bruce and Joyce Walker, *Discovering Intimacy* (Austin, TX: Relationship Press, 2002).

Chapter 5: Impossible Dreams Made Possible
1. http://en.wikipedia.org/wiki/Angels_in_the_Outfield_(1994_film)

Chapter 6: Taking Your Dreams Out of the Wait
1. Dondi Scumaci, *Designed for Success: Ten Commandments for Women in the Workplace* (Lake Mary, FL: Excel Books, 2008).
2. Blue Letter Bible. "Dictionary and Word Search for *dynamis (Strong's 1411)*". Blue Letter Bible. 1996-2012. 26 Mar 2012. http://www.blueletterbible.org/lang/lexicon/lexicon.cfm?strongs=G1411
3. Blue Letter Bible. "Dictionary and Word Search for *dynamis (Strong's 1415)*". Blue Letter Bible. 1996-2012. 26 Mar 2012. http://www.blueletterbible.org/lang/lexicon/lexicon.cfm?strongs=G1415
4. Erik Rees, *S.H.A.P.E.: Finding and Fulfilling Your Unique Purpose for Your Life* (Grand Rapids, MI: Zondervan, 2006).

About The Author

Shuronda Scott has over 25 years of corporate and ministry experience. She has served on the staff of Covenant Church, a large multi-campus church in the Dallas/Fort Worth area for over 14 years in various ministry roles including Small Groups Ministry Coordinator, Director of Counseling and Restoration and currently as the Women's Leadership Development Director. As a Christian Counselor, she had the opportunity to ministry to hundreds changing and impacting their lives through the grace of God's healing and restoration.

No matter what her role, Shuronda is passionate about helping others remove limitations (within) that releases them to walk in their fullest potential and possibilities (without).

As a speaker, author and certified life coach, Shuronda influences in many REALMS including the marketplace. She currently oversees the Reign Makers Business Women's Network at her church as well as hosts a quarterly Power Luncheon of business owners, executives and other business and community leaders who are making an impact in the marketplace.

For more information on her coaching or ministry visit WalkingInPossibility.com or connect with her on:

Facebook/shuronda.scott
@ShurondaScott – Twitter
Linkedin.com – Shuronda Scott

Discover Your Roadmap of Possibilities

Are you ready to walk in possibility and realize your dreams? Contact Shuronda regarding the right coaching solution designed to help you walk in God's amazing possibilities for your life.

Mapping Your Personal Success
(Shaping Your Life Message)

Mapping Your Professional Success
(Developing Your Professional Profile)

Mapping Your Business Success
(Turning Your Passion Into Profit)

Walking in Possibility 12-Week Coaching Intensive
(4P Leadership Success Strategies and myPossibility Network)

Healing the Brokenhearted Dreamer
Conferences and Intensive Weekend Encounters

Experience the life-changing conferences and events that are bringing healing to the brokenhearted dreamer. You can move beyond the devastation and loss of shattered dreams. Discover the power of God's healing that releases you to dream again! He truly gives beauty for ashes.

For additional information and conferences dates visit us at shurondascott.org.

What Client's are Saying about Shuronda

"The Lord led me to Shuronda back in 2007. She has been my Coach for both my nonprofit organization and my for profit business. I am so grateful for the accountability and guidance she gave to me to strengthen my weakness. With each new level I achieve, Shuronda has been an instrumental piece to the backbone of my success."

Karla Armstrong, CEO/Director/Coach
mommyStrong™
"Change Your Mind, Change Your Life"
www.mommystrongdfw.com
214-282-8359

"Shuronda has been a blessing to my organization, both as a business consultant and a strong spiritual influence. We are better at servicing the families that come to us for help because of her commitment to detail and passion for her fellow man."

Darlene Greene, Founder & Executive Director
Ina Mae Greene Foundation-For My Sisters
"Because the Road to Safety Should Not be a Dead-End"
www.inamaegreene.org

"Shuronda Scott's coaching has made a remarkable difference in my life and ministry. She provides an amazing vehicle for looking at your life, setting realistic goals, and mapping out an executable plan of action. She helped me to see my life's work from an empowering new vantage point."

June Evans, Author, Speaker, Teen Empowerment Coach and Founder of Treasures By You Training Systems, www.juneevans.com

"Shuronda Scott with DFS Coaching Solutions helped us hone in on strategic developmental areas for our business. This provided a clear vision with goal setting for the direction and growth we desired to achieve. She helped us prepare, fine tune, and market our business to gain new clientele. She taught us effective strategic communication on how to provide a presentation that will deliver the desired perception and favorable results. We are thankful for the wisdom and years of knowledge she willingly shares and how she encourages us to take hold of all opportunities. Thank you, Shuronda for doing what you do!"

Jason & Kim Scott, CEO and Vice President
Scottfree Design / Haute Hats
"Live Free Forever"
www.scottfreedesign.com
214-995-2232

"Shuronda Scott at DFS Coaching Solutions has been my coach for over four years and my life has changed for the better. She has coached, mentored, and guided me through some of the toughest life changes like transitioning from my career as a forensic chemist to successful business women. I will touch the lives of billions with the confidence and knowledge she has imparted to me in every aspect of my life as a woman, wife, and child of God. I am thankful for her and how she has changed my life and many others."

Michelle Curry-Cobb, Owner
Events by Design & Demand
www.eventsdesigndemand.com

DREAM JOURNEY NOTES

DREAM JOURNEY NOTES

DREAM JOURNEY NOTES

DREAM JOURNEY NOTES

DREAM JOURNEY NOTES